ALLEN BREED SERIES

M000098259

The Allen Breed Series examines horse and pony breeds from all over the world, using a broad interpretation of what a breed is: whether created by the environment where it originally developed, or by man for a particular purpose, selected for its useful characteristics, or for its appearance, such as colour. It includes all members of the horse family, and breeds with closed or protected stud books as well as breeds and types still developing.

Each book in the Allen Breed Series examines the history and development of the breed, its characteristics and use, and its current position in Britain, together with an overview of the breed in America and worldwide. More difficult issues are also tackled, such as particular problems associated with the breed, and such controversies as the effect of the show ring on working breeds. The breed societies and their role in modern breeding policies are discussed.

BOOKS IN THE SERIES

The Appaloosa
The Arabian Horse
The Coloured Horse and Pony
The Fell Pony
The Hanoverian
The Irish Draught Horse
The Morgan Horse
The Mule
The Quarter Horse
The Trakehner
The Welsh Mountain Pony

The Morgan Horse

A classic head: Tarryall Gene Thiery ('Maestro'), Britain's most influential performance and show sire to date, seen here wearing a traditional Morgan show bridle.
(*Photo by J. Bulmer, courtesy British Morgan Horse Society*)

ALLEN BREED SERIES

The Morgan Horse

Sally Spencer

J. A. Allen

London

British Library Cataloguing in Publication Data
A catalogue record for this book is available from the British Library

ISBN 0-85131-599-2

Published in Great Britain in 1994 by
J. A. Allen & Company Limited
1 Lower Grosvenor Place
London SW1W 0EL

Series editor Elizabeth O'Beirne-Ranelagh
Book production Bill Ireson
Printed in Great Britain by The Longdunn Press Ltd, Bristol

Contents

Page

ACKNOWLEDGEMENTS   viii
PREFACE   x

1 Introduction   1
2 Justin Morgan and his horse Figure   3
3 The development of the Register and Morgan Horse Club   17
4 Influential breeders   26
5 The characteristics and contribution of the Morgan horse   63
6 The Morgan in America today   73
7 Introduction of the Morgan to Great Britain   81
8 Profile of Morgan horses in Great Britain   93
9 The Morgan worldwide   118
10 The Morgan in sport   130
11 Conclusion   151

BIBLIOGRAPHY   153
INDEX OF HORSES' NAMES   155

Front cover: UVM Dexter in the Vermont homeland of the Morgan. (*Photo courtesy Charles and Charlotte Ross, Taproot Morgan Horse Farm*)
Endpapers: Morgan horses at Herts County Show. (*Photo by Nicola Sutton*)

Acknowledgements

No book of this nature can be brought to fulfilment without assitance from many and varied sources. It is the result of a united effort, generously made by Morgan horse lovers around the world. From them I received an abundance of support, knowledge through conversation, literary information, letters and photographs. To them I extend my sincere gratitude and appreciation for their help and patience, kindness and hospitality.

To those who contributed to a collection of almost 300 photographs, many thanks for a memorable nightmare, which after some painful selections of my own I passed on to plague the book's designer. Where no attribution is given in the photo captions, the photographs were kindly provided by the owners of the horses pictured. To those who provided facts, information and the all-important reference material, thank you for broadening my horizons and those of this book.

A special thanks to my friends Dr Trudy Mackay, North Carolina, whose logical thinking helped greatly, and to Sue Brotherstone, Edinburgh, who in the early stages gave me a much needed Thesaurus, now very worn. Grateful thanks to my editor, Liz O'Beirne-Ranelagh, whose encouragement never ceased, especially regarding my use of the Thesaurus! Thanks also to Rhona and David Bertram for endless cups of coffee and the use of their computer.

Contributions which crossed the Atlantic were particularly overwhelming. I am indebted to Anne Boorman Canavan, Tennessee, for her numerous mailings; she finally landed on my doorstep herself, weighed down with heavy historic volumes, and needed a big mug of tea. To Betsy Curler, Vermont, of the Lippitt Club Archives, for her remarkable generosity, and to Tracy Holloway who worked on behalf of the American Morgan Horse Association, Vermont. Many thanks to Robert Morgan, California, and to Gail Perlee, Arizona, who enriched this book and my desire to go Westward ho.

Very special thanks to Jennifer DuBois, New Hampshire, and Morgan Sport Horse Association members everywhere for actively supporting Morgan performance with a capital 'P'. For generous hospitality, shared recollections, discussion and literary gifts, many thanks to Marilyn Childs, Kenneth Telford and my dear friend Anne Cole, all of Vermont. To Sherry Ackerman Ballou and Charles and Charlotte Ross of Vermont whose knowledge and experience, kindness and enthusiasm was so freely given, much appreciation.

On this side of the Atlantic no words can express my gratitude to Nancy Hedley-Dent, whose encouragement and friendship knows no bounds, and to Sarah Baker, now back in Canada, for her listening ear and revelations. To Gillian Eyre, retiring from dedicated service as Registrar for British Morgans, a well-deserved thank you. Many thanks to Morgan horse owners in Britain and on the European Continent for their valuable contributions, and to dear Tom for his inimitable support and tolerance regarding telephone bills. Finally, this book is dedicated to the late Lee Ferguson with great affection, and to Morgan Horses past and present whose individual magnetism cannot help but surface and grow no matter what the circumstances.

The late Lee Ferguson, inspiration to Morgan Horse owners worldwide.

Preface

The history of the Morgan breed is intertwined with that of the American people. American history is extremely significant for the evolution of a breed of specific type and character, a breed that has diligently served the needs and whims of its owners for over 200 years.

Jeanne Mellin Herrick, a noted Morgan authority, artist and author, precisely describes the importance of breed type today in the Foreword of her book *The Complete Morgan Horse*:

> It cannot be stressed enough that the Morgan is a type breed. His type is his hall-mark and his heritage. Without it we have just a group of horses that, with train-ing, are versatile but are Morgan in name only. The 'Morgan look' is a distinctive thing. As you familiarize yourself with this look, you will come to understand why it is so important for breeders and judges to have a thorough comprehen-sion of Morgan type and character.

The Morgan is, without doubt, a survivor. It is difficult not to romanticize or to expound upon the breed's virtues. Ths story of the breed's origins was immortalized by Walt Disney in his film *Justin Morgan Had a Horse*, based on the much loved novel of the same name, written by Marguerite Henry. Both the novel and the film have inspired the minds and hearts of people, young and old alike, and encouraged them to seek a Morgan horse of their own.

In this book I have tried to portray the true performance value of the breed, its strength, courage and agility. In addition to basic fact, the historic portions of the text cover the nature of the various environments in which the breed found itself, and the resulting requirements, to increase an understanding of those times.

For reasons of space there are a large number of people and horses, instrumental in the development of the breed, who have not been mentioned, and for this I apolo-gize.

1 Introduction

The Morgan is the oldest light horse breed developed in the United States of America. The breed's unique quality is the fact that each breed member can trace its origin to a single foundation sire, the Justin Morgan horse. His first recorded owner was Thomas Justin Morgan, the man who introduced the stallion to the people of Vermont, totally unsuspecting of the value and attention his horse would be given in the future. To him the horse was known as Figure.

Figure, who later became known as Justin Morgan, was foaled in 1789 in Springfield, Massachusetts. It was the same year that the new Constitution of the recently united States came into force. A fresh page of American history was begun when George Washington was inaugurated the first President to serve the nation. Never before had such a task faced any man. Appearing in front of a considerable crowd who had come that April to witness him take the oath of office in New York City, standing on the balcony of the Federal Hall, he said: 'My station is new. I walk on untrodden ground.'

This statement heralded the birth of a nation, a new era into which the Morgan unwittingly slipped and trod purposely shoulder to shoulder with a struggling people in their quest for freedom, justice and liberty.

The physical distinctiveness of the Justin Morgan horse, his soundness, energy and industry, his tractable temperament, his cheerful spirit and his remarkable ability to bless his offspring with his own characteristics and qualities, made him a legend in his own lifetime. Through three of his sons the breed was founded, later to be the only registered breed perpetuated by the US Government and celebrated as the 'Pride and Product of America'.

The state of Vermont, first settled in 1720, was the home of Justin Morgan for 30 of his 32 years. It became the capital of the breed. A proud and competitive spirit in support of the Morgan and his offspring manifested itself in the Vermonters. Stories of the great horse and his family were passed mainly by word of mouth, probably embellished with each narration. News of Vermont's treasure spread.

After the death of Justin Morgan, for those who set out to trace his origin and to record his description, his life and his offspring, the stories made wonderful listening, but the conflict of memory and conjecture quite often thwarted progress. However, one man, Daniel Chipman Linsley, set a precedent for other researchers to follow when his book *Morgan Horses* was published in 1857. Up to that time printed breed information was usually only to be found in local newspapers and agricultural journals in the form of advertisements, articles and general correspondence. Linsley's book had no personal bias as he did not own Morgan horses. His respect for the breed's 'extraordinary hardiness, speed and endurance from severe use' when compared to other types of horses motivated him to research the breed extensively and to publish his findings which he 'deemed too valuable to be lost'. Linsley's description of the Morgan in the preface of his book is particularly valuable because it describes the breed as it appeared only 36 years after Justin Morgan's death.

> If size is, as is claimed by some, the measure of power, it will be found that form is the measure of action. Too much size is, indeed, incompatible with rapid and continued action.
>
> The most casual observer of a good Morgan horse, is conscious that he sees a peculiar animal. His short, light, rapid step, point to the great muscles which give him motion. His prominent, clear, eager eyes, set wide apart, testify to his courage and docility – while his clean, light head, carried high, with short pointed ears, gives grace and elegance to every motion.

Morgan horses have contributed to many facets of American life. In the past they helped pioneer the West, worked on ranches, served as much needed Cavalry mounts, pulled freight from township to township, worked the soil and cleared the land. They were also popular as fashionable riding and harness horses. Morgans were highly influential in the development of the trotting horse industry worldwide.

The breed's versatility today is seen in practically every modern capacity, ranging from therapy programmes to ranching, general family and pleasure use, to a wide variety of show and sport disciplines.

2 Justin Morgan and his horse Figure

The man

Morgan was born on 28 February 1747 to Isaac and Thankfull Day Morgan of the West Parish of Springfield, Massachusetts. He was the eighth of eleven children, four of whom died in infancy. Morgan came from an established family of yeoman farmers, his great grandfather, Miles Morgan, having settled in Springfield in 1643. During the frontier years the Morgan family had contributed significantly to the cultivation of the Connecticut Valley and were instrumental in helping to develop the area's facilities, such as schools, libraries and churches.

By the age of 24 Morgan had purchased 22 acres of land from his father. Eventually, due to ill health thought to be tuberculosis, he was unable to undertake hard labour. Morgan was fortunate, however, that he had acquired other skills and was well educated for his time. 'Mr Morgan was very much liked because of his gentility, fine manners and sterling character.' He was described as being 'upright, industrious and poor' (Earl R. Farshler, *American Saddle Horse* (1934)).

In December 1774, the year West Springfield officially became a town, Morgan married his first cousin, Martha Day. Their first child was born in 1776.

Over the years Morgan supplemented his earnings by teaching music and the art of penmanship, highly regarded skills at that time, and he was a composer of some merit. Morgan loved the church and music and amidst his life as a farmer, a teacher and a horseman he found time to write a number of musical compositions that attracted attention in his own lifetime, as have his surviving compositions in the present day. Thomas Justin Morgan not only earned a place in history because of his outstanding horse Figure, but also as a musician and psalmodist of undeniable skill.

Morgan's love of well-bred horses involved him in breeding, training and ownership. He leased several thoroughbred-type stallions during his time in West Springfield and advertised them for stud in the local newspapers: Sportsman in 1778, Diamond in 1783, and True Briton, or Beautiful Bay as he was otherwise known, in 1785. Justin Morgan, no doubt, had an 'eye' for a good horse, and being of a sensitive and long-suffering nature, he most likely had a great affinity with them. He lived 25 miles south of Hartford, Connecticut, the main trading centre for the buying, selling and breeding of quality horses.

By 1788 Justin Morgan was in a delicate state of health. Not only had he lost two of his children but he faced crippling tax burdens. These heavy taxes were a result of massive debts accrued from the Revolution and they threatened small landowners with potential ruin. Vermont had asserted its independence several years earlier on 17 January 1777. Morgan moved his family to Randolph, Vermont to join family and friends long since settled in the new republic and endeavoured, through great hardship, to make a new life.

The Justin Morgan horse

Figure

The foaling date of Figure has been open to speculation. Daniel Chipman Linsley estimated it as 1793, whereas Col. Joseph Battell (1840-1915), who undertook the enormous task of creating the first Morgan Register in 1894, believed it to be in 1789. His belief was based on an advertisement for Figure that appeared in *Spooner's Vermont Journal* published in April 1793. In 1794 and 1795 stallion advertisements for Figure also appeared.

The understanding is that Justin Morgan had sold Figure's dam in foal before he moved to Randolph and later returned to the area to claim her colt in lieu of payment of a debt owed to him. He then returned to Randolph in time to advertise the colt in 1793. Whatever the tale, the colt known as Figure was eventually to make an indelible mark upon the equine history of America.

Beginnings

It is now accepted that by 1793 Figure had arrived at the stable of Justin Morgan and as a four year old was advertised at stud. The ailing Justin Morgan trained Figure, whose spirit was great and bountiful, to go kindly and willingly so that children and ladies could ride and drive him with ease. Morgan did not own the horse for long. By 1795 his wife had died and his children were fostered, his illness preventing him from providing an adequate living to support them. He leased Figure to a farmer, Robert Evans, of Randolph, for $15 annual fee. Evans, a poor man with a large family to support, farmed his own land and supplemented his income by logging, clearing land and building fences for others.

Justin Morgan, from a woodcut in Linsley's *Morgan Horses.*

Figure, with no other horses to assist with the heavy toil, set to work alongside Evans and together they tackled the rough and unyielding Vermont landscape. Evans was amazed by the stallion's strength and courage and word soon reached the neighbourhood that Figure was a force to be reckoned with. Farmers and loggers would often collect after a hard day's work for their glass of cheery refreshment, perhaps cider beer or brandy, and amuse themselves by organizing competitions: walking, trotting and pulling matches with their horses. Fortunately for his fame, but perhaps not after a heavy day's toil, Figure excelled and impressed the locals immensely, and bigger and more arduous tests of strength, speed and endurance were devised. In lantern light on narrow tracks with inebriated human competitors one hesitates to imagine what the horses experienced. Understandably Figure's fame spread.

In 1796 Figure was advertised in the *Burlington Mercury* by Samuel Allen of Williston, whose stable Figure had stood at during part of the 1795 breeding season. On 22 March 1798 Justin Morgan died. Recent research has discovered that Morgan probably exchanged his prize horse, Figure, for 100 acres of land belonging to Samuel Allen in an endeavour to provide for the future of his children. In the early part of the 1796 breeding season Allen, who seemingly was disappointed with the lack of demand for the stallion's services, sold him to William Rice, then of Randolph. The reason for Allen's disappointment could well have been that he was located on the west side of the Green Mountains, and respect for Figure's blood existed mainly on the east side at that time. Rice had the horse for a matter of weeks before selling him on to Jonathan Shepard of Montpelier, who stood him for the remainder of the season. Records show that on 14 February 1798 ownership of Figure was transferred to James Hawkins, also of Montpelier, Vermont. After that it is not known exactly who owned Figure or where he went until 1801, when he appears in the ownership of Robert Evans, who no doubt had eagerly awaited the opportunity to buy him. Once more Figure undertook heavy and arduous work with Evans, but despite the industry of his horse, Evans sank into debt and was sued by his creditors, and in 1804 Figure was transferred into the ownership of Col. John Goss of Randolph, who had paid Evans' debts.

According to Linsley, Col. Goss was not a horseman himself. He gave Figure to his brother David, whose farm was near St Johnsbury. David Goss owned Figure for

The residence of David Goss, St Johnsbury, Vermont, built before 1805. From *Home Library Illustrated*, Middlebury, Vermont, 1904. (*Photo courtesy Elizabeth Curler*)

seven years, and though he was employed on the farm quite regularly, Figure experienced a life of relative ease compared to his previous homes. He was constantly in demand as a mount for parades and official public functions. His nervous energy and spirited step, combined with his great gentleness, intelligence and tractablity, enamoured him to all who had contact with him. Figure was still matching his abilities in competition with other horses. During this period his stud career was at its best. Many of his offspring had matured, growing like their sire and becoming known, even then, as Morgan horses. As a consequence of this great success the demand for his services was high and he returned to the stable of John Goss, still in the ownership of David Goss, to stand for the 1807 breeding season. He also stood for part of the season in Claremont, New Hampshire. It was during this period that his most influential son, Sherman Morgan, was sired.

In 1811 Figure, at the age of 22, was sold by David Goss to his son Phillip, who took the horse back to Randolph where demand continued for his breeding services. This was around the time when the famous Bulrush Morgan was sired. Perhaps people who owned Figure in his later years became nervous of losing their investment, as his purchase price and earnings had remained significantly high; Linsley wrote, 'those who owned him seemed eager to get rid of him, for fear that he should die on their hands'.

Hard times

After the 1811 breeding season, according to Linsley, Figure was sold to Jacob Sanderson. Sanderson sold him to Jacob Langsmade, a freight haulier who demanded value for money from all his equine purchases, needing suitably sound and courageous individuals to haul freight over the abominable roads and tracks in all weathers. Langsmade put Figure to work pulling wagons in a six-horse hitch between Windsor and Chelsea. One can well imagine the gruelling conditions and it is no surprise that the little horse may have lost an immense amount of condition for the first time in his life.

Respite

In poor condition Figure was sold for a small sum to Joel Goss. (I have found no evidence to suggest whether or not he was a relation of the other Goss family.) He kept him in partnership with Joseph Rogers who lived near the ferry in Claremont, New

Hampshire. This is where Figure stood at stud for the 1814, 1815 and 1817 seasons, siring his notable sons Woodbury and Revenge. He was then sold to Samuel Stone, a past stud handler of Figure. Approximately two years later Figure was sold to Levi Bean, spending his last years on the farm of Clifford Bean, about three miles south of Chelsea. In the winter of 1821 Figure was running out with other horses, apparently without shelter from the severe weather conditions. It is reported that he sustained a flank wound, left untreated. As a result of infection and old age Figure breathed his last.

On reflection

Those who reportedly saw Figure during his last years remembered him as still possessing a youthful, exuberant appearance and attitude to life, free from blemish and entirely sound. It is sad to think that he should die in such a neglected state, but reflects the times in which he lived, for the pioneering people of Vermont were unlikely to fare much better themselves. Their struggle was continuous, with few resources to nurture an animal past its productive life.

In these early days horses were often called after the surname of whoever owned them at the time. This practice relayed the individual horse's whereabouts and possible background. Figure, known as the Goss horse whilst in the ownership of David Goss, also became known respectfully as the Justin Morgan horse, and his resulting offspring were called Morgan horses. This established, in part, a record of a particular and valued type of horse, its area of origin, and its pedigree. It was a fitting tribute to the man, Thomas Justin Morgan, who had introduced to his community a sire of such usefulness and worth at a time when such a resource was most needed.

However, all was not lost in that winter of 1821. The tough little horse who had been able to impress many during his lifetime was destined to impress others by leaving his stamp on his fine offspring and the legacy of the father 'Figure'.

Foundation pedigree and surrounding influences

Lack of recorded evidence meant that the pedigree of the Justin Morgan horse remained in question for quite some time, causing much debate and varied interpretation of phrases associated with his breeding, such as being of the 'best blood' or described as the 'Dutch horse', the two phrases often thought to be synonymous. Morgan researchers and dreamers have had a wonderful time, teased with limited concrete evidence. Especially compelling is the desire of many individuals involved with other breeds to suggest that their favoured breed was the forefather of the Morgan. Obviously this could be true to some extent, as the breed developed over generations from the roots of a single sire and many and varied dams.

However, as far as Justin Morgan himself is concerned a pedigree has been accepted by the Morgan world. The basis of this pedigree is the breeding programme of British royalty, from the time of Charles I of England, through Oliver Cromwell to Charles II and the return of royalty to the English throne. Many famous breedings are recorded in this pedigree. The phrase 'best blood' is found in a letter from Justin Morgan Jr to the *Albany Cultivator* in 1847. Discussing the sire, Justin Morgan, he concluded: 'My father always spoke of him as a horse of the best blood.'

This phrase, taken in a modern context, could have been applied to the major imports of Arab and Thoroughbred stock, primarily from Britain. The early development of the Morgan is not unlike that of the Thoroughbred. Thoroughbred ancestry has always been subject to speculation, as some believe that there is no concrete evidence that the famous foundation sires, the Godolphin Arabian, the Byerley Turk, and the Darley Arabian, were of pure Arabian descent. Whatever the story, the blood was potent and manages to prove itself repeatedly, despite many and varied crosses.

One interesting factor pointed out by Peggy Jett-Pittenger in her book *Morgan Horses* (1967) is that

> the short back of the Morgan indicates a high percentage of Oriental blood. Not only are the Arab's individual vertebrae shorter in length than the common horse, they are also fewer in number. Similarly many Morgans have one less than the usual six lumbar vertebrae and one fewer pair of ribs than the usual 18 or 19. According to H. H. Reese of the Bureau of Animal Industry, at post mortem examination General Gates 666, Donald 5224, Dude 4673 and a weanling colt by Troubadour of Willowmoor 6459 were found to have only five vertebrae.

If you compare the description by the veterinary surgeon Omer, who saw the Godolphin Arabian in his prime, to that of Linsley's description of the Morgan horse, you will notice the similarities:

> his shoulders were deeper and lay further into his back than any horse I have yet seen. Behind the shoulder there was a very small space before the muscles of his

9

loin rose extensively high, broad and expanded which were inserted into his hindquarters with greater strength and power than in any horse I believe ever seen of his dimensions.

The official sire of Justin Morgan, True Briton, was said to have been stolen during the Revolution from Col. James De Lancy, a British Army officer, at King's Bridge, near New York City. True Briton then travelled round the country under other names such as Traveller and Beautiful Bay, eventually standing at stud at the stable of the singing master, Justin Morgan, in 1785. Some speculation that True Briton was of Welsh breeding is based on the fact that it was a popular name in that breed. Little is known about the dam of the Morgan horse, said to be by Diamond out of a Sportsman daughter. She was reported to have been a light bay in colour, with heavy mane and tail, and was foaled in 1784 at West Springfield and owned by Justin Morgan.

The Morgan horse was also referred to as the 'Dutch horse', a phrase found in an earlier letter from Justin Morgan Jr to the *Albany Cultivator* in 1842. The possible reason for this is that the Dutch had imported draft horses considered unsuitable for riding to New Netherlands, a settlement established in 1626 by the Dutch West India Company which stretched up the valley of the Hudson River and on to Long Island. Its main town on Manhattan Island was called New Amsterdam. The colony became British in 1664 and the New Netherlands became the English New York in 1667. But many New Englanders continued to call anything brought in from that area 'Dutch'. Apparently the draft horses resembled the Morgan quite closely but would not have had the same turn of speed. Friesian horses had also been imported and were considered prize animals, as they possessed great trotting capabilities and good looks and were temperamentally sound. The Friesian had been crossed with Arab and Andalusian blood to add quality and refinement, and was also in great demand as a sire in Western Europe. The breed was used extensively in Britain to improve trotting stock.

Another breed said to be of Dutch origins was the Narragansett pacing horse. During the early part of the eighteenth century the majority of horses kept in and around the remote communities of New England were pacers. This gait was thought to be not only faster but safer for covering the inevitably rough ground. The breed numbers were unfortunately allowed to dwindle for various reasons: enormous export to the West Indies, the improvement of roads, and the fact that the Narragansett was unsuitable for draft. The Narragansett horses were celebrated for speed, endurance and fleetness. Not only were they worthy entertainment when racing, but they were skilled on rough terrain and undaunted by distance. They were a safe ladies' mount and a valued possession, becoming one of the forefathers of the American Saddlebred Horse.

When discussion concerning the pedigree of the original Morgan horse was at its most heated, some people maintained that a Canadian breed had been integral to the Morgan. It is supposed that the Narragansett Pacer and the Canadian Pacer were closely related but the Canadian horses had qualities so marked as to make them recognizable as a special breed. They were a little heavier, were hardy and compact, and were thought to have been a cross between French horses of Norman and draft type. They did not possess the speed of many roadsters of the time. Grandsons of the Morgan horse travelled to Quebec and it was said that the improved qualities of the Canadian horse were due to these individuals, although other commentators intimated the reverse. As horses travelled extensively from area to area, it is likely that mares of French origin from Canada were bred to Morgan sires in and around Vermont. According to Kenneth Telford, out of only ten mares put to Justin Morgan whose origins were indicated, two 'were said to be French, one from Canada, the other presumably so, being respectively the dams of Gordon Horse 582 and Bulrush Morgan 6'. However, one theory which jeopardizes this supposed link, according to Mabel Owen, was that the bay colour so strong in the early Morgans was virtually unknown amongst the predominantly chestnut French Canadians. Very interestingly, an article writtein in 1991 by Laird O'Brien from Toronto, Canada, highlighted a breed now recognized as the Canadian Horse, which was declared a national breed by Parliament in 1909, and which resembles the old type of Morgan remarkably closely both in colour and form. This old breed is now rare with a population of approximately 1000, apparently finding its origins in New France (Quebec, Canada) in the mid 1600s.

Thus various theories and opinions abound, but what can be gained is a detailed portrayal of the times in which the original Morgan horse and his descendants lived and the need for their endurance and stamina, coupled with tractable temperaments. No doubt the breed evolved from a combination of the most potent and successful blood of those times.

Three most influential sons

Justin Morgan undoubtedly sired a magnificent number of colts and fillies. However, mare records are almost non-existent due, largely, to the fact that more attention was paid to stallions, with regard to their breeding abilities and form, and the income derived from their use at public stud. Research has unearthed authentic accounts of six sons of Justin Morgan that were kept at stud. The three most influential ones, Sherman, Woodbury and Bulrush, will be discussed briefly here. They are particularly important because each is acknowledged for producing his own family line known for specific traits, and when these were later combined the characteristics and attributes of the original Morgan were reinforced. Geographical limits and personal preference resulted in the initial segregation of these three main sons and their families, enough at least to warrant separate classes at the Vermont State Fairs in the 1850s.

Although the similarities of the three families were more obvious than their differences, each had its loyal support group. Some early breed authorities have suggested that three generations passed before the families were intermingled, but this has since been contested and families may have been interbred earlier on. However, we cannot doubt the pride that existed in each separate family, as family identity is still of importance in Morgan breeding today.

Sherman Morgan

Sherman was a bright red chestnut bearing a white hind sock and a small facial stripe, bred by James Sherman of Lyndon, Vermont. He was thought to have been foaled around 1808 or 1809, and matured to slightly under 14 hands, weighing approximately 950 pounds. His dam was said to be of quality Arab or Barb blood, probably a British import. She possessed a golden coat and a spirited nature, and displayed speed, beauty and refinement. Sherman inherited the strength and build of his sire. His head was finely chiselled, featuring small ears and rather small eyes but they were prominent with a kindly expression. His only fault was a slightly swayed back, sometimes inherited by his offspring though this did not affect their soundness in any way.

Like all his brothers Sherman Morgan changed hands frequently, standing in many different locations in Massachusetts, Vermont and New Hampshire and producing approximately 40 entire sons during his breeding career. He was often used for farm work and haulage, pulling a freight sledge in winter with a gelding half-brother between Lyndon and Portland, Maine. He was a spirited individual, well remembered for his tractability, kind disposition and matchless stamina and soundness. Sherman died on 9 January 1835 leaving his sons and their progeny to spread his fame

throughout the country, the Western Territories and overseas. They were also instrumental in influencing the foundation of other American breeds.

The Shermans were unsurpassed as harness horses and most prolific between Newbury and the Canadian border. Chestnut was the predominant colour. Sherman's descendants in direct line far exceed those of the other Morgan sons, principally through the trotting hero Ethan Allen 50, by the celebrated trotting horse sire Black Hawk, Sherman's most famous son. It is said that every Morgan alive today traces to Sherman by one or more lines, through Ethan Allen and Mansfield. Mansfield, foaled in 1920, carried over 50 crosses to him. Sherman Morgan was thus the most influential of all Justin Morgan's sons.

Woodbury Morgan

Woodbury was foaled in 1816, in Tunbridge, Vermont, bred by Lyman Wight. He was a dark chestnut with an off hind stocking and a facial stripe running from mid face to upper lip. The tallest of the three, Woodbury weighed approximately 1000 pounds. He exuded quality, with his lean straight head and large expressive eyes set wide apart. His ears were small, his nostrils very large and full; his body compact,

13

Woodbury
Morgan.
Drawing by
Jeanne Mellin-
Herrick.

strong and deep, his chest broad. Woodbury's tail was set high and only ten inches long, docked in the fashion of the day.

The breeding of his dam has never been traced but she was reported as being a dark bay standing at 15 hands, weighing near to 1100 pounds. She lacked compactness and paraded a finely shaped head carried high, an excellent chest, shoulders and hindquarters. Her description was 'strung out and flat ribbed' though her overall appearance was reported as pleasing. She walked with a rapid step and trotted and paced at good speed in harness.

Woodbury inherited much of his sire's zeal and courage, creating a demand for his services as an excellent saddle and parade horse, enjoying the noise and brightly coloured sights of such occasions. His playful disposition did not deter Woodbury from being an accomplished harness horse. Woodbury passed through several ownerships and in 1836, after the death of his owner, lawyer Peter Burbank, he was sold at public auction and destined for Gainsville, Alabama. Reports suggest that Woodbury was shipped out from Boston, but suffered illness or injury resulting in his death. Whatever the circumstances there are no records of any stock in Alabama.

Woodbury's most famous son was Gifford Morgan. Gifford, out of a Morgan-type mare, retained the type of his grandsire and was much admired as a parade horse, becoming a very popular sire of some 1300 foals. His most famous son, Green

14

Mountain Morgan (also known as Hale's Green Mountain, Young Woodbury and Old Green Mountain Morgan), is recognized as the breed prototype, his likeness appearing on the American Morgan Horse Association's registration certificates. The Green Mountain Morgan died at the age of 30 leaving a heritage of great worth to the Morgan breed.

The Woodburys were most numerous in central Vermont, excelling as saddle horses, their attitude ideal for parades. The Woodbury line would have died out but for the horses bred by J. H. Peters and Son of Bradford, Vermont. Ethan Allen 2nd, sired by Peter's Morgan, a grandson of Green Mountain Morgan, saved the day, creating a distinguishable line of his own. He sired Ethan Allen 3rd, Headlight Morgan (highly instrumental in the development of the Western Working Morgan) and Croydon Prince, a foundation sire of the Lippitt Morgan strain.

Bulrush Morgan

Bulrush, a deep bay with no white markings except a few white hairs on his forehead, was foaled in 1812, bred by Moses Belknap of Randolph, Vermont. He stood approximately 14 hands and weighed 1000 pounds. The breeding of his dam remains

Bulrush Morgan.
Drawing by Jeanne
Mellin-Herrick.

15

unknown but she was a dark bay with a heavy mane and tail, a long low-set neck but a pleasing enough head. Compact and large of bone she apparently lacked the refinement and quality of the dams of either Sherman or Woodbury, and did not portray that much sought after spirit, yet she was an adept trotter. Belknap had acquired her from a teamster, and sold her on in foal to Mr Gifford (later the breeder of the Gifford Morgan) with the agreement that the foal be returned to Belknap should Gifford not purchase it separately. Gifford declined the extra payment, hence the colt was returned to Belknap.

Bulrush's conformation differed from that of his brothers. He was larger boned, with flat and broad joints, and though his back was not ideally short his muscular development was immense. His temperament was calm and less vivacious, but his powers of endurance and speed were extraordinary. His tail was docked like Woodbury's and he displayed a luxuriant knee-length mane.

Because of the combination of traits Bulrush inherited from his sire and dam – speed, level-headedness, heart and endurance – Bulrush became a much sought after and successful trotting horse sire. Since these traits were crucial to trotting races, which were rapidly gaining popularity and invited financial benefit, Bulrush's use as a Morgan breed sire was limited. However, 16 sons were retained as stallions, 13 of them bay. He sired the Randolf horse, foaled in 1820, this son inheriting his sire's abundant mane and remarkable endurance. The Randolf horse, when only two, sired Morril, the founder of the celebrated Morril family of trotters, one of which was Fearnaught, the world's greatest trotting stallion of his day who trotted the mile in 2 min. 23 sec. Bulrush, after experiencing quite a number of different homes, spent the last years of his life in the ownership of F. A. Weir of Walpole and died at the remarkable age of 36 in 1848.

The Bulrush male line is extinct but his qualities have passed through the dams of many exceptional horses. Many of the mares of Western breeders were of Bulrush descent, but few if any of their colts were registered. The tail male line of descent of the Bulrush line existed for some time through Sun Down Morgan 7388, foaled in California in 1933. He traced to Morril but was bred mainly to mares of no defined breed. The same applies to Red Flash 8416, also foaled in California in 1940, as he was used principally on Thoroughbred mares culled from racehorse production.

3 The development of the Register and Morgan Horse Club

Daniel Chipman Linsley

Daniel Chipman Linsley was the first man to research the Morgan breed extensively. He was born on 17 April 1827, the son of Charles and Martha Linsley, farmers of the Middlebury, Vermont district. Although Linsley was never to breed Morgan horses himself, his father had bred two early stallions. Vermont horses were increasing in demand throughout New England and New York, known for their style and speed as excellent carriage and tradesmen's horses.

By 1847 Linsley, on completion of his education at Middlebury College, began work surveying for the Rutland and Burlington Railroad. His career as a civil engineer entailed travelling in the south and west. During these journeys he studied the horses of the various regions and came to the firm conclusion that the hardy, compact, stylish and durable Vermont horses were far superior.

So enamoured was he with his conclusions, that Linsley embarked on a detailed study, researching the Vermont Morgans' various family backgrounds and descent from the original sire, Justin Morgan. At this time the Vermont Agricultural Society, within their sponsorship programme, offered an award for topical essays of the day. Linsley submitted his findings in essay form and was awarded the first premium on 15 January 1856. His continued enthusiasm resulted in the publication of his essay as an illustrated book, *Morgan Horses*, in 1857, containing information of some 240 stallions.

Linsley led an accomplished life as a civil engineer, researcher, historian, politician and editor of the *Vermont Stock Journal*, first published in Middlebury in January 1857. His diligence and dedication led to breed recognition and preservation, for which all supporters of the Morgan are indebted. He died on 7 October 1889.

In his book, *Morgan Horses*, he describes from his researches the foundation breed sire, Justin Morgan:

> The original, or Justin Morgan, was about fourteen hands high, and weighed about nine hundred and fifty pounds. His colour was dark-bay with black legs,

mane and tail. He had no white hairs on him. His mane and tail were coarse and heavy, but not so massive as has sometimes been described; the hair of both was straight, and not inclined to curl. His head was good, not extremely small, but lean and bony, the face straight, forehead broad, ears small and very fine, but set rather far apart. His eyes were of medium size, very dark and prominent, with a spirited but pleasant expression, and showed no white round the edge of the lid. His nostrils were very large, the muzzle small, and the lips close and firm. His back and legs were his most noticeable points. The former was very short; the shoulder blades and hip bones being very long and oblique, and the loins exceedingly broad and muscular. His body was rather long, round and deep, close ribbed up; chest deep and wide, with the breast bone projecting a good deal in front. His legs were short, close jointed, thin, but very wide, hard and free from meat, with muscles that were remarkably large for a horse of his size, and this superabundance of muscle exhibited itself at every step. His hair was short, and at almost all seasons soft and glossy. He had a little long hair about the fetlocks, and for two or three inches above the fetlock on the back-side of the legs; the rest of the limbs were entirely free from it. His feet were small but well shaped, and he was in every respect perfectly sound and free from any sort of blemish. He was a very fast walker. In trotting his gait was low and smooth, and his step short and nervous; he was not what in these days would be called fast, and we think it doubtful whether he could trot a mile much if any within four minutes, though it is claimed by many that he could trot in three.

Although he raised his feet but little, he never stumbled. His proud, bold and fearless style of movement, and his vigorous, untiring action, have, perhaps, never been surpassed. When a rider was on him, he was obedient to the slightest motion of the rein, would walk backwards rapidly under a gentle pressure of the bit, and moved sideways almost as willingly as he moved forward; in short, was perfectly trained to all the paces and evolutions of a parade horse; and when ridden at military reviews (as was frequently the case), his bold, imposing style, and spirited, nervous action attracted universal attention and admiration.

He was perfectly gentle and kind to handle, and loved to be groomed and caressed, but he disliked to have children about him, and had an inveterate hatred for dogs, if loose always chasing them out of sight the instant he saw them.

When taken out with halter or bridle he was in constant motion, and very playful . . . He was a fleet runner at short distances . . . In harness the Justin

18

Morgan was quiet but full of spirit, an eager and nimble traveller, but patient in bad spots; and although for a long time steadily engaged in the heavy work of a new farm, his owner at that time informs us that he never knew him refuse to draw as often as he was required to, but he pithily adds: 'I didn't very often have to ask him but once, for whatever he was hitched to generally had to come the first time trying.'

This uniform kindness at a pull, was one of the striking characteristics of the horse, and the same trait may be observed in the greater part of his descendants.

Joseph Battell

Joseph Battell, also a native of Middlebury, Vermont, and a student of the town's College, was born 12 years after Daniel Linsley, on 15 July 1839. He not only continued Linsley's documented research of the breed, but went further still to produce *The Morgan Horse and Register*, printed in 1894, therefore giving the breed official standing. His monumental land and farm donations to the United States Government established an official Morgan breeding farm, which though now divided is still in existence today. Battell, himself a Morgan breeder, also provided the farm's foundation sire, General Gates 666.

Battell's unquenchable love of the Morgan, and his joy of stylish roadsters and trotters, provided the motivation for eight years of exhaustive research culminating in Volume I of *The Morgan Horse and Register*. A man of means and leisure, Battell travelled extensively to verify horses, pedigrees, old papers and documents and the lionised tales of old timers. Thousands upon thousands of letters were written and received; in short no stone was left unturned, no expense spared. Linsley's premium essay was reinvestigated and applauded for its accuracy.

Battell's unadulterated love of the roadster and trotter, however, precipitated a thorny problem as far as Morgan purists were concerned. Battell categorized the breed into three sections: family horse, farm horse, roadster and trotter, of which he supported the latter most strongly.

Morgan blood had given edge, turn of speed and endurance to trotting stock, desired requirements at the time, and in this guise the Morgan was recognized as a prime contributor to the development of the trotter. Many such individuals were celebrated in the name of the breed, which helps explain a deterioration of efforts to breed the purest of Morgan blood in certain localities. Battell derived quite a number of pedigrees from the American Trotting and American Saddle Horse records, Morgan blood an accepted feature of both. Battell remained resolute in his belief that roadster and trotting ability were the factors for assessing performance levels. This is clearly indicated in the Register, which relays the recorded trotting times of countless individuals.

Battell became the largest landowner in Vermont. An assiduous conservationist, he left thousands of acres to the State of Vermont, Middlebury College and the United States Government for that specific purpose. The altruistic nature of Joseph Battell combined with the remarkable efforts of Daniel Linsley left a great legacy for other Morgan breed devotees. Without this contribution the breed would probably have failed to attain the position of distinction it occupies today.

The Register and the Morgan Horse Club

The Register

Volume I of *The Morgan Horse and Register*, a massive 996-page, well-illustrated work containing pedigrees, explicit details of thousands of horses, letters, individual achievements, and many relevant accounts, notices and documents, was followed by Volume II in 1905, also prepared by Battell. This volume included information from the preceding work, plus new additions.

In Volume I Battell spelt out the rules of admission to the Register:

> Any animal in either of the following classes is eligible to register in the MORGAN REGISTER.
> 1.   Any meritorious stallion or mare that traces in direct male line to the original Justin Morgan Horse and has at least one sixty-fourth of his blood.
> 2.   The produce of a sire and dam both registered in the MORGAN REGISTER.

For Volume II of the Register a new rule was entered, making eligible for registration all horses tracing through the dam to Justin Morgan and possessing 1/32 of the blood.

Joseph Battell died in January 1915, prior to the completion of Volume III.

Middlebury College, receiving the work as part of Battell's estate, completed and published it later that year.

The Morgan Horse Club

The Morgan Horse Club was founded in 1909, 15 years after the publication of Volume I of the Register. Upon publication of Volume II in 1905, many seasoned Vermonters expressed increasing concern for breed purity and stability. The Vermont Morgan had, in part, survived despite the inclusion of diluted Morgan blood of road-

Detail from 'Morgans going to the fair', by George Ford Morris, formerly owned by Henry G. Darling, Lyndonville, Vermont. (*Photo by Bill Orson, courtesy Lippitt Club Archives*)

21

ster and trotter type in the Register. Fashionable trends too were taking their toll, as horses of increased speed, style and refinement for ridden and harness use were sought. Those concerned felt that the blood of the Vermont Morgan would be diffused with the blood of other breeds and performance types, hence suffering a serious loss of the Morgan's distinct characteristics. These influences may have depressed Morgan devotees at the time, but the ultimate challenge was presented by the epoch-making advancement of the railroad and automobile, reducing the demand for the Morgan as a working horse, a use which had depended on the breed's unique attributes.

The Vermont State Fair in White River Junction, Vermont, was the venue for the Club's first meeting. The Fair had been revived in 1907 by Maxwell Evarts (1862–1913), a founder member of the Morgan Horse Club. Sixty members attended that day, 23 September 1909, 31 attending a later meeting held in Hartford, Vermont, on 27 November 1909, to vote in the constitution and bylaws and elect a board of fifteen governors and five vice presidents.

The purposes of the Club were the retention of breed type and characteristics; to formulate a breed standard; to encourage registration; to promote breed classes and enlist judges of similar vision; to offer prizes to stimulate showing and breeding; and to promote a close unity amongst breeders and members. Success seemed guaranteed. Club meetings continued to be held at the Vermont State Fair and breed class entries increased from 90 in 1909 to 187 in 1912. Sadly this leaping progress was to be curtailed.

The Register and the Club united

With two links of the chain secured to ensure the beginnings of breed preservation and recognition, more were needed over the ensuing years to support population growth and to survive times of decline.

C. Chauncy Stillman, secretary of the Morgan Horse Club since its formation, purchased *The Mogan Horse and Register* from the Middlebury College administration on 29 November 1919 and instigated the Register's incorporation, according to the laws of the State of New York, under the new title, *The American Morgan Horse Register*. Offices were established in New York City, all expenses of these and the Register being maintained by Stillman until his death in 1926. It was at this time that a serious decline of breed numbers and Club membership was becoming evident.

Hard roads and the increasing use of automobiles were the main contributors to

22

change from general light horse use, especially carriage horses for which the Morgan breed was noted. With fewer than 40 Club members in 1926, concern was voiced as to whether the register could be maintained. Charles Augustus Stone, an active breeder of Morgan horses, was one of the most noted and influential Club benefactors. He had a history of long service with the Morgan Horse Club and took a keen interest in the health and integrity of the Register, generated by his friendship with Mr Stillman.

Stone offered the Club temporary assistance. This offer was accepted for over 30 years! He undertook the responsibilities of the offices and Register. To receive the assets – the Register as incorporated by Stillman – the Morgan Horse Club itself had to be incorporated, which was duly done on 1 November 1927, and the Register received. After Mr Stone's death in 1941, his son Whitney, long-time treasurer of the Morgan Horse Club Inc., continued to provide the Club's quarters and sponsorship of the Register until 1961.

Frank B. Hills warrants mention here. He has been described as 'meticulous' and 'fastidious', and he became the backbone of the Register and Club. He became estate manager for C. A. Stone in 1925 and was assigned the intricate work of the Registry. Mr Hills was also executive secretary of the Club from 1927 to 1961. It was he who presented plans for the Club's incorporation. Mr Hills compiled Volume V of the Register to coincide with the 150th anniversary in 1939 of the birth of the Justin Morgan horse, and further compiled Volumes VI to VIII, his final volume being published in 1960. Hills witnessed an annual growth of registrations from fewer than 100 to over 1000 a year by the time of his death in 1961.

Registration requirements tighten

On 1 January 1921, as seen in Volume IV of the Register, the following requirements for registration became effective.

RULE I: The produce of a sire and dam both registered in the American Morgan Horse Registry.

RULE II: To register any horse in the American Morgan Horse Register which is not the produce of a sire and dam both registered therein, application with full particulars should be made to the Executive Committee of the Morgan Horse Club whose decision will be final.

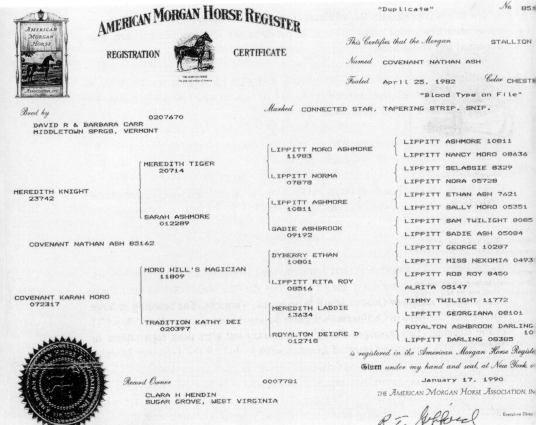

Registration document as it looks today

In Volume VI those horses admitted under Rule II were designated an X preceding their registration number. Rule II was rescinded in 1948:

Effective January 1, 1948: Only the progeny of a sire and dam both of which are already registered in the American Morgan Horse Register will be accepted for registration.

A new rule was passed in 1962 to eliminate registration of coloured horses. Some of these variations occur today, a result of previous outcrossings, but are rare. It is known at the White Rule:

> Effective April 7, 1962: No horse shall be eligible for registration which has a wall eye (lack of pigmentation in the iris) or natural white markings above the knee or hock except on the face.

Numbers beginning with 0 apply to mares and geldings registered in Volumes II–IX. Since Volume X, geldings have been registered in the stallion section of the Register. The American Morgan Horse Association does not maintain a part-bred Morgan register. The Half Morgan Register, a division of the American Part-Blooded Horse Registry, was begun in 1940 and continues today.

Breed revival

By the early 1940s health had been restored to registrations and Club membership. Shows and activities increased, the climax being the National Morgan Horse Show first held at the Upwey Oval in South Woodstock, Vermont. The breeding of large numbers of Morgans in California took place during the years covered by Volume VI of the Register. This upsurge suffered a temporary lull after peak registrations in 1947, due to a downward trend of living standards, but by the 1960s the Morgan Horse Club Inc. was on a sound financial footing. In 1964 a trust fund of $125,000 was organized to guarantee the future of the Register. The Morgan Horse Club Inc. is known today as the American Morgan Horse Association Inc., and though it has endured some rather turbulent times, it supports the breed and membership with an all-encompassing interest, as will be discovered in a later chapter.

4 Influential breeders

The United States Morgan Horse Farm

The United States Morgan Horse Farm was established primarily as a result of the efforts of Senator Redfield Proctor, Chairman of the Senate Committee on Agriculture, in 1904. The Morgan breed, on the whole, had been dispersed and was in decline despite the endeavours of dedicated breeders. Vermont faced the potential loss of an integral part of its history, not just an exceptional breed of horse. Senator Proctor proposed that the United States Department of Agriculture initiate a Morgan horse breeding programme to supplement studies undertaken by the Vermont State Experiment Station at Burlington, concentrating on the reproduction and nutrition of livestock.

By 1907, the venture authorized, a small band of mares was selected and acquired. Some, however, were not registered and two from Kentucky were of Saddlebred breeding. Vermonters did not agree with the Department's choices, especially those from Kentucky. The Department's requirements which the mares had to meet were height, ranging from 15.1 to 15.3 hands, pure trotting paces, style and action, good conformation and to be 'well bred along Morgan lines but registration in the American Morgan Horse Register will not be necessary'.

It had already been established that Morgan type was better retained in the smaller Morgans. However, those involved with the new Morgan breeding programme were resolute in their belief that breed survival depended on making a successful transition from the economic needs of the past to the recreational needs of the future. With increased height, improved paces (eliminating a tendency to mixed or irregular gaits), retention of the breed's abundance of endurance and spirit and good conformation, the Morgan, as an improved saddle and general performance horse, would be the ideal and practical solution.

In 1907, furnished with a generous land donation from Joseph Battell of some 400 acres (the farm later possessed almost 1000 acres), the new breeding programme had the facilities in which to flourish. The land lies in Weybridge, two miles from Middlebury, Vermont, and became the base of one of the most remarkable and far-reaching breeding programmes within the Morgan breed. The band of seven mares, two fillies and the stallion General Gates 666 were installed the same year.

Life-size bronze statue of
Justin Morgan donated by
C. C. Stillman in 1921.
(*Photo courtesy AMHA*)

The farm's programme for breeding horses with the required characteristics and refinements, but sometimes lacking a purity of blood as desired by Vermonters, brought heavy criticism. In response to this the Farm justified their decisions by saying that outside infusions of blood were acceptable in so far as they originated from a similar lineage to that of the Morgan.

The US Bureau of Animal Industry, Circular 163, 1910, by George Rommel, Chief of the Animal Husbandry Division, stated:

27

Blood lines cannot yet be drawn hard and fast in Morgan breeding. We must select type first of all, and by so selecting we will with each succeeding mating intensify the type and improve the pedigree. If the Morgan horse is to be regenerated, horses must be bred not pedigrees . . . The test of the worth of a pedigree is the animal it produces. If follows, therefore, that a consideration of pedigree by a judge in the show ring is a reductio ad absurdum.

General Gates

General Gates was bred by Joseph Battell and foaled in 1894. At 13 years of age he was acquired by the 'Government' Farm to head the stud, which he did until his death in 1920. Battell's penchant for the fast trotter led him to admire Lord Clinton, bred in Kentucky, an able trotter attaining a time of 2:08 (when individually timed) and winning races in 2:10. However, Lord Clinton posed a problem: he was a gelding. Battell's answer was to purchase his sire and dam, Denning Allen 74 and Fanny Scott, to repeat the breeding and produce General Gates, full brother to Lord Clinton.

Denning Allen possessed an acceptable pedigree, tracing back to Ethan Allen 50, one of the most celebrated American trotters of all time. Fanny Scott, however, was of quality thoroughbred breeding. General Gates differed from his race-structured brother quite considerably. He was more compact, possessing a semblance of old Morgan type.

General Gates, foundation stallion of the Government Farm. (*Photo courtesy AMHA*)

General Gates was described by W. F. Hammond, Superintendent of the US Morgan Horse Farm, in a 1911 Vermont Agricultural Report:

> His selection was not made wholly on his individuality as a Morgan of modern times, but on his ability as a sire of the desired type. His colour is black; foaled May 6 1894, and stands 14 hands 2½ inches high, weighing 1000 pounds when in trim. . . From my stand-point, I firmly believe the name of General Gates will go down through all time as one of the greatest sires of the Twentieth Century.

General Gates sired a total of 53 foals for the Farm. He was an excellent road horse and cavalry type. His foals were sold to various parts of the country to establish new lines and contribute to others. His third foal, Bennington 5693, was perhaps his most successful and contributed not only to the production of remount horses but to the programme at the US Morgan Horse Farm.

Bennington and Artemisia

Bennington, foaled in 1908, was the first colt by General Gates. His dam Mrs Culvers 3711, purchased from Kentucky and registered in the American Saddle Horse Register (ASHR), was by Harrison Chief, a well-known progenitor of the Saddlebred breed. Her dam was Billie, who provided traces of Morgan blood through Cabell's Lexington 1223, also registered in the ASHR. After two initial breedings, one at two and one at three years old, Bennington was sent to stand at the Fairlee Remount Centre across the state.

In 1919 a high percentage Morgan mare was brought to Bennington's court at the Remount Centre for what has since been described as a 'fortuitous' breeding. The mare was Artemisia 02731, owned by A. Fullerton Phillips, but leased at that time by William B. Sanders. The combined genes of Bennington and Artemisia laid the foundations of a breeding programme that would ultimately spread worldwide and become so sought after that according to Dayton Sumner, an authority on the breed, in 'The Mare who Made Bennington Famous' (*Morgan Horse Magazine*, July 1990):

> the 'golden cross' of Bennington and Artemesia proved so successful that today more than 90 percent of all living Morgans trace to them. Many other lines which derive from Bennington were also from mares of similar breeding.

Bennington (*above*), an outstanding sire for the US Morgan Horse Farm. This is not his best shot but shows his 'cavalry' look; Artemisia (*opposite, above*) photographed in her old age; Mansfield (*opposite, below*) pictured at about 5 years old. (*All photos courtesy AMHA*)

Artemisia had a total of ten foals by Bennington. Twenty-three other mares bred 67 foals by him.

Mansfield

The 'golden cross' was the inimitable Mansfield 7255, foaled 16 June 1920. By 1922 his potential was recognized and he was purchased by the Farm. Artemisia was also purchased and Bennington, not surprisingly, was recalled to stud duties at the Farm from the Remount Centre. Together father and son shared stud duties until

Bennington's death at the age of 28. Mansfield carried on, siring a total of 146 foals, and became a major influence in the Farm's extensive line-breeding programme.

Farm policy was to use the Morgans for general farm and utility work as well as showing and performance events. Mansfield was no exception, winning numerous championships and performing well under saddle and in harness, whether single, pair or team. His last public appearance was at the South Woodstock Morgan Show in 1942 at the age of 22. He won the Justin Morgan Horse class which included saddle and harness races, a ridden section and the pulling of a stone boat weighing a minimum of 500 pounds.

His full brothers, Querido 7370, Ulysses 7565 and Canfield 7788, also became noted sires. Querido went to the prolific breeder Roland G. Hill's Horseshoe Cattle Company ranch in California, and later to Hawaii. Ulysses stood with Dr W. L. Orcutt, the Remount service and the US Morgan Farm. He produced the well-remembered stallion Ulendon. Canfield assisted the programmes of both the University of

Canfield, showing his resemblance to his brother Mansfield. (*Photo courtesy AMHA*)

Connecticut and the US Morgan Farm and sired the Grand Champion stallion, Panfield, used in the breeding programme of the University of Connecticut.

From breedings to Mansfield came sons and daughters founding veritable dynasties of their own. Mansfield made clear the importance of using mares of sound Morgan breeding and perhaps restored respect for the extraordinary qualities of the blood of the original Justin Morgan horse. A more uniform type of horse was emerging, exclusively 'Government', making a sizeable contribution to the performance of Morgan horses in the show ring and sporting pursuits.

The University of Vermont Morgan Horse Farm

The Government decision to cease funding of the Farm in 1950 led to the reorganization of the Morgan breeding programme. In 1951 it was agreed by the General Assembly of Vermont that the operation should continue under the ownership and directorship of the University of Vermont and the State College of Agriculture but with reduced numbers. A portion of the stock was sold by sealed bid, and prices were attained that clearly showed respect for 'Government'-bred Morgans. Others were sent to University programmes, two stallions to the Bureau of Indian Affairs, and the remaining livestock and assets, including 20 mares, 5 fillies, 4 stallions and 5 foals, were transferred to the University of Vermont (UVM).

Difficult times were ahead. Major Farm maintenance was required, funds were restricted and a lack of interest was noted for the true perpetuation of the breed and its contribution to the people of Vermont. In 1959 the Farm survived another threat of closure after national and international protest. In 1963 and 1971 further difficulties were overcome, thanks to the support of a more than generous and dedicated Morgan community. Insufficient funding also limited the Farm's use of outside breeding stock. Ted Davis contributed the services of Upwey Ben Don and Roger and Anna Ela contributed those of Orland Vigildon.

Upwey Ben Don 8843 has been described as 'incomparable'. Foaled in 1943 he was by Upwey King Benn, by Upwey King Peavine X8074, son of American Saddle Horse registered parents. Upwey King Benn was out of Audrey, a daughter of Bennington and Carolyn. Ben Don's dam was Quietude by Troubadour of Willowmoor, a stallion used extensively by the US Farm between 1919 and 1923, producing 33 foals. Quietude's dam was Ruth, and like Carolyn was of good Morgan breeding. Ben Don was known as an excellent sire of broodmares.

Orland Vigildon was sired by the great Ulendon, by Ulysses, sired by Bennington

Upwey Ben Don. (*Photo courtesy AMHA*)

and out of Artemisia. Vigildon was out of the high percentage registered Lippitt mare Vigilda Burkland who is also famous for two other Ulendon sons, Orcland Leader and Vigilendon, later gelded but a true show horse. Both Upwey Ben Don and Orcland Vigildon were excellent sires of show horses and performance horses.

Through time strict methods of evaluation resulted in a uniform type of Morgan being bred at the UVM Farm. In the early 1990s, the farm stands approximately six stallions, breeds 15 to 20 mares annually and is involved with the training of 15 to 30 young horses. Concentration is on producing and preserving 'traditional Morgan type and character, while breeding quality individuals for amateurs and families'. The Farm has also played a dominant role in the show ring and continues to produce Morgans of that calibre and quality today. Since its inception the Farm has been credited with placing Morgans worldwide, highlighting the breed's versatility and powers of performance in all spheres.

UVM Farm Morgans are also involved with various equine-related research projects and educational programmes linked to the University and the Vermont community. Animal Science students have weekly sessions at the Farm using laboratory facilities, and students are also provided with hands-on experience of horse management and training. The Farm enlists the help of a small staff and depends upon the community for volunteer helpers, working still within the confines of a restricted budget. During the height of the tourist season, from May to October, the UVM Farm welcomes thousands of visitors from all over the world who want to absorb Morgan breed history and meet the Morgans first hand. Visitors can also take pleasure in surveying the rich limestone pastures and abundant acreage of trees, offering an especially splendid display in autumn. Appealing architecture can be seen in the white Victorian barn built in 1878 by Joseph Battell, which stands not far from the impressive statue of the horse Justin Morgan, donated by C. C. Stillman in 1921.

The years since 1906 have witnessed major developments within the Morgan breed. The work of the Farm as a federal venture was concentrated primarily on establishing a light horse breed suitable to modern-day requirements and of com-

The magnificent white Victorian barn built in 1878 by Joseph Battell. (*Photo by the author*)

mercial value, as well as on preserving a unique nationally developed breed. Besides their studies of nutrition and reproduction, performance testing was introduced. Even though this was not on a massive scale it did much to highlight the Morgan's natural attributes and draw further attention to the retention of breed type, endurance, stamina and, not least, the breed's remarkable temperament. Between 1919 and 1926 the War Department sponsored 300-mile Endurance Rides to encourage durable light horse breeds and to understand better the skills and care required for such strenuous activity. Morgans fared very well and continue to do so today. The Farm was also instrumental in aiding the development of shows, by entering large numbers of Farm-bred horses in the various classes, and so helping to attract further interest to the breed. In short, the efforts made by the Farm gave focus to a breed that might not otherwise have stood the test of time, and established a stable base from which other breeders could progress. However, it must be recognized that most of what has been accomplished is due to the enlightened contribution of the Morgan community itself, which supported the breed through its most crucial times of development and continues to do so to the present day.

The Lippitt Morgan

The Lippitt Morgan is a specific family strain within the breed. All Morgan horses recognized as Lippitts by the Lippitt Club and Register descend through numerous crosses to a 'cornerstone' stallion, Ethan Allen 2nd 406, bred by the Peters family of Bradford, Vermont in 1877. Ethan Allen 2nd traced directly to the original Morgan sire, Justin Morgan, his pedigree containing three crosses to the famous Hale's Green Mountain Morgan 42. Therefore today the purebred Lippitt continues to be bred along nineteenth-century lines, containing no twentieth-century out-crosses of any kind, the product of a purposeful 100-year linebreeding programme to retain not only purity of blood but the attributes and characteristics which are original and fundamental to the Morgan.

Standards of the Lippitt Morgan

The Lippitt Club set down the following standards:

> The ideal Lippitt Morgan ranges from 14.1 to 15.1 hands; he has a short head, great width between the eyes, and a well crested neck of medium length, which

Hale's Green Moutain Morgan 42, ancestor of the Lippitt Morgan.

A good example of a Lippitt Morgan mare, Madrona Samantha (Meredith Bilirubin x Woodstock Tabitha), born 1984. (*Photo by Janet Heineck, courtesy Ed and Mary Rein*)

comes out of the top of a long, well-laid back shoulder and blends smoothly through the withers into a well-sprung deep body. The back is short and smoothly joined to the hindquarters; the croup is long, wide, and slightly sloping, balancing the front quarters. The legs have long forearms, thighs and gaskins, and short cannons, with medium length pasterns corresponding to shoulder angle. A compact horse with substance of bone combined with refinement, nervous yet controllable energy influences his powerful, rapid, and elastic gaits.

Confusingly, not all horses bearing the prefix 'Lippitt', the produce of Robert Knight's breeding programme, qualify as Lippitt Morgans as defined today, being the result of outcrossings to other family lines.

The specific Morgans chosen by the Lippitt Club in 1971 to constitute the foundation stock of the purebred Lippitt Morgan were:

STALLIONS	MARES
Croydon Prince 5325 (1890)	Bonnie Jean 1343 (1895)
Rob Roy 4483 (1893)	Polly Rogers 02109 (1896)
Donald 5224 (1904)	Lucille 01557 (1902)
Bob B 5282 (1905)	Rose of Sutton 02232 (1904)
Welcome 5702 (1907)	Bridget 02852 (1904)
Sir Ethan Allen 6337 (1909)	Emily 03026 (1909)
Sealect 7266 (1921)	Evelyn 0684 (1909)
Bilirubin 7462 (1925)	Hippolyta 03222 (1910)
	Nancy 03553 (1911)
	Trilby 02532 (1911)
	Susie 03786 (1915)
	Lippitt Trixie X-04695 (c.1916)
	Croydon Mary 02900 (1917)
	Lippitt Sallie 04565 (1918)
	Lucinne 04542 (1918)
	Hannah 03196 (1919)

There would be a larger selection of horses on the list above if a greater number of early breeders had kept their original stock 'pure'. However, in spite of many and

Bell Marea, an early Lippitt mare. (*Photo courtesy Lippitt Club Archives*)

various outcrosses old blood is still present in numerous pedigrees. One good example of this is found in the Brunk breeding programme (see below).

History of the Lippitt

We have become aware, in earlier pages, of the concern voiced by some about purity of blood and breed attributes, opposed to those who would mould the Morgan breed to modern-day requirements of size and refinement and use the blood of other breeds to do so. Without adherence to purity and detail on the part of a breeding minority, the 'cornerstone' of the breed would certainly have been lost.

In the Lippitt Morgan we have the truest example of the Morgan as being wholly descended from the remarkable influence of a single sire. Once more we find affluent and principled individuals being influential in preserving the Morgan breed, with a clarity of purpose which would impress any breed purist.

A. Fullerton Phillips is recognized as the primary preserver of this family strain. Originally from eastern Pennsylvania, eventually to settle in Windsor, Vermont, around 1915, Phillips sought Morgan horses of original type, ability and purity among the nestled homesteads and hamlets of Vermont and New Hampshire, with the intention of establishing a specialized breeding programme.

From 1907 Phillips amassed his choice herd, and also became a founding member of the Morgan Horse Club in 1909. Between 1910 and 1927, the year he died, Phillips judiciously bred 41 Morgans, painstakingly recording pedigrees, his views and research in abundant notes which still survive today.

Of the Morgans Phillips either owned or bred, 30 are listed amongst the first 55 horses to be registered in the Lippitt Register. Some of them are amongst those selected by the Lippitt Club as the foundation sires and dams of the Lippitt family. The sires were Croydon Prince, Welcome, and Rob Roy; the mares Rose of Sutton, Bridget, Emily, Hippolyta, and Nancy, constituting a remarkable contribution from one man. A. Fullerton Phillips is also recognized for his inadvertent contribution to the US Government breeding programme, by leasing the famous mare, Artemisia, to W. B. Saunders, who subsequently bred her to Bennington and produced the 'golden cross', Mansfield.

Robert Lippitt Knight (1883-1962), however, is the man most immediately remembered and associated with the Lippitt Morgan, as his breeder's prefix, 'Lippitt', stands fast today, identifying the family line and paying tribute to his successful endeavours in inbreeding and linebreeding. He steered the Lippitt safely through the rigours of the second quarter of the twentieth century until his death in 1962.

Robert L. Knight resided at Lippitt Farm in Hope, Rhode Island. He was a successful businessman and breeder of quality Ayrshire cattle. In 1921 he purchased the Green Mountain Stock Farm, Vermont, to enlarge this interest, but in 1927 the farm also became the home of two stallions and four mares purchased from the Phillips estate, plus a small number from other sources. The stallions, Ashbrook 7079 (Croydon Prince x Nancy), the cream of Phillips' breeding programme, and Moro 7467 (Welcome x Polly Rogers), originally christened Eureka by Phillips, were the major influences in Knight's breeding programme. Moro unfortunately died early in his career, but is noted especially for John A. Darling (x Bridget), Lippitt Kate Moro

Lippitt Rob Roy (*above*); and (*below*) Ashbrook, the mainstay of Robert Knight's breeding programme. (*Photos courtesy Lippitt Club Archives*)

(x Croydon Mary), and Lippitt Moro (x Croydon Mary). Ashbrook, on the other hand, enjoyed an extensive career, siring his own dynasty. The blood of Ashbrook was used predominantly in Knight's inbreeding and linebreeding programme, in the care of his farm managers. Ashbrook sired the famous stallion Lippitt Ethan Ash (x Trilby) in 1928, to become Knight's favourite pleasure driving horse when he visited Vermont. Even though living at a long distance from his Morgans, Knight was involved with them to a large degree and he also served on the Board of Directors of the Morgan Horse Club. He was not an enthusiastic exhibitor, showing his horses little until the last years of his life.

In an attempt to repopularize the breed, Knight agreed to exchange breedings with the US Government Farm. In 1938 and 1939 he sent his choicest mares to be bred to Mansfield. They were Lippitt Kate Moro, foaling Lippitt Morman and Lippitt Mandate, which both became excellent sport horses and sires; Lippitt Trilby Ash, foaling Lippitt Byfield and Lippitt Trilman; and Nekomia, foaling Lippitt Nekoman and Lippitt Scofield. Some authors have stated that much to Knight's resentment he was the only one to fulfil the agreement. However, new information made available

Lippitt Moro Ash (Lippitt Moro x Lippitt Sally Ash), a product of Knight's breeding, at his retirement ceremony with Tex Talley. (*Photo courtesy Betsy Curler*)

to me indicates that the US Farm did breed a few mares to Knight's stallions with at least two offspring being registered. It seems that the US Farm's choices were based on size, as they selected the taller but not the best of Knight's stallions, Lippitt Sam and Lippitt Selassie. In addition, the Government Farm sent poorer quality mares and placed all the blame on the Lippitt contribution when the resulting foals were disappointing.

In June 1952 Knight, apparently disillusioned with the Saddlebred influence in the breed, held a dispersal sale, much of his stock staying in New England. Quickly regretting his decision, and especially missing his old horse Lippitt Ethan Ash, Knight attempted to repurchase his original stock between 1953 and 1960 and resume his breeding programme. However, many of the Morgans Knight had bred were not for sale and the quality of his new breeding programme perhaps did not meet his original standards of excellence. Knight also allowed his horses to be trained for and exhibited at shows in the new tradition, though this did not prevent his criticism of showing and training techniques, especially overlong feet and weighted shoes. Soon after Knight's death in 1962 the second and final herd dispersal took place, with the

Royalton Ashbrook Darling, sired by Knight's favourite stallion, Lippitt Ethan Ash. Foaled 1950, owned and driven by the late Dana W. Kelley. (*Photo courtesy Lippitt Club Archives*)

auction of his horses and equipment bringing viewers, buyers and hopefuls from all over the United States, and the prices of his stock well reflecting the valued contribution he had made.

There are a significant number of farms today which carry out pure Lippitt breeding as their sole enterprise and also some which, as well as breeding purebred Lippitts, also outcross to other Morgan lines. Advertising and pedigrees, however, can often confuse the newly interested potential breeder or purchaser of the valuable family strain of Lippitt Morgans. Contact with the Lippitt Club is the simplest way in which to attain the information required.

The Lippitt Club

After the death of Robert Lippitt Knight, owners, breeders and admirers of the Lippitt were motivated to preserve the strain, and began planning ways in which this could best be achieved. Breed promotions were organized to increase public understanding and recognition of the importance of Lippitt breeding.

In comparison to the total Morgan population the Lippitt family was a mere drop in the ocean, yet its contribution to other Morgan families is very significant. The present Lippitt population is reported to be approximately 1000.

The Lippitt Club was formed in 1971 and today supports a worldwide membership in Canada, Sweden, Great Britain and across the USA.

A Lippitt Register was privately published by Kenneth Telford and Vol. II of this has been accepted by the Club as its official register. Vol. II (1986) gives 'A Complete Listing of All Morgans Defined by the Lippitt Foundation Stock as Lippitt Morgans from 1890 to 1980, Together with 7-Generation Pedigrees of Lippitt Ancestors and Computed Percentages of Justin Morgan's Blood for All Horses'. This register also contains a number of photographs of foundation stock and forewords by Telford.

The Club sponsors numerous promotional programmes including the Lippitt Country Show, held each August, the Lippitt Driving Day and the 25-Mile Open Competitive Trail Ride, Vermont Youth Amateur Show, the Lippitt of the Year Award, a dressage day, the Allen's Major Show Award (the saddle/harness, log programme), and it initiated the Justin Morgan Standard Class at many Morgan and Open shows, receiving much popularity.

The continuous research and development of the Lippitt Club Archives is quite outstanding, providing interesting literature and copies of photographs relating to a

huge assortment of past Lippitt breeding stock, themes and places to anyone express-
ing their interest.

The Lippitt contribution

Disparaging remarks have at times been passed about the amount of inbreeding the
Lippitt strain has undergone. But other Morgan bloodlines have experienced more
inbreeding than the Lippitt, one example being the UVM Morgans, many of whom
were highly inbred to Bennington under the Directorship of Dr Balch. However, with
the Lippitts, linebreeding has been practised more than inbreeding. Marshall N.
Winkler, Lippitt breeder and efficacious promoter of its versatility and competitive
capabilities against other breeds (especially in driving, from singles to four in hand),
supports the strain in an article entitled 'A New Look at an Old Family', circulated
by the Lippitt Club and printed in the *Morgan Horse Magazine*:

> The Morgan breed fancier should encourage the effort to retain this Green
> Mountain strain free from outcrosses. All breeders who use this principle of
> hybrid vigour or heterosity must first create inbred lines as a foundation. I know
> of no other breed where there is a family to compare with this line in the amount
> of inbreeding already completed. Horses because of their relatively slow breed-
> ing would take several lifetimes to establish the true lines essential for hybrid
> programmes. All the disappointments would need to be lived again. The period
> of lowered fertility, nervous instability and the various other weaknesses that are
> dredged up from the depths of the genetic pool would have to be endured and
> selected out until finally a degree of similarity is achieved in the gametes. This
> stage has been achieved already in the Lippitt.
>
> There are several stallions and mares bearing the Lippitt prefix that are
> themselves the result of outcrosses and although they bear the principle – hybrid
> vigour in the first generation, would not be useful in the perpetuation of the
> homozygote line.
>
> Although I personally prefer the strain pure, much of its value to the breed
> lies in the potential that exists for utilizing the undeniable fact of its unique pedi-
> gree. The inbred line exists because of several unrelated circumstances and all
> but disappeared but for the dogged determination of Robert L. Knight. Romantic
> considerations alone saved it, the devotion to the ideal of 'purity' and the horror

Dyberry Robin and daughter Envi's Doris (half Lippitt), driven by owner Dr Elmer Searles. (*Photo courtesy Lippitt Club Archives*)

of the 'mongrel', but for whatever reason, it is with us in its undiluted state and it should not be allowed to disappear into the general genetic pool of the Morgan breed.

Many Morgans famed for their performances as show or sport horses and breeding stock have been of 50 per cent Lippitt breeding. Over the last 50 years horses with either dams or sires of Lippitt breeding have created lines of their own, such as Ulysses, sire of the great Ulendon; Lippitt Pecos, revered Western States sire; Pecos, sire of remarkable show horses, his line very prolific in Great Britain; Orcland Vigildon and Orcland Leader, sires of exceptional show and performance stock.

Purebred Lippitts continue to make an enormous contribution to the Morgan breed,

Pecos (*above*), a famous sire by the Lippitt stallion Cornwallis out of Hepatica; Orcland Leader (*below*), by Ulendon out of the Lippitt mare Vigilda Burkland. (*Photos courtesy AMHA*)

Royalton Ashline at an AMHA Driving Event in 1979. (*Photo by Phaneuf Gurdziel, courtesy Clara Hendin and Betsy Curler*)

excelling in every pursuit and in family use. The most notable collection of achievements are those of the stallion Royalton Ashline (Royalton Ashbrook Darling x Royalton Elenora).

In 1983 the American Morgan Horse Association Inc. (AMHA) introduced a Sport Horse Award which not only defines what versatility is all about but also demands a standard that most horses and owner/rider/drivers would be hard pressed to achieve. To attain this award participants have to achieve bronze medallions in five areas of AMHA-designated Open Competition: open show classes, dressage, competitive or endurance trail riding, combined training (eventing), and carriage driving. These must be achieved in competition with all breeds of horses, not just Morgans. When I first started writing this book in 1990, only one horse had attained the award, namely Royalton Ashline 23744, owned by Clara Hendin, formerly of Vermont, now living in West Virginia. 'Roy' took from 1979 to 1986 to earn his medallions culminating in the award. This was no feeble challenge and says as much for the efforts of his owner and friends as it does for the horse.

This seal brown stallion, foaled in 1972, enjoyed sidesaddle, western and hunter-jumper classes, trotting races, parades and a torrent of etceteras, accumulating first placings and winning 30 show-ring Championships and Reserve Championships in 13 different disciplines. He was trained and competed 90 per cent of the time by amateurs and women.

No wonder Ms Hendin had to move to Virginia, no doubt to house all of his trophies and ribbons. 'Roy' cut a legendary figure of enormous proportions, a huge individual standing 14.2 hands! Sadly Royalton Ashline died in a road accident in the summer of 1991.

Morgans Westward Ho

Morgan horses in the Midwest

Morgan horses rapidly travelled westwards, easily capable of coping with the varying needs and demands of areas other than their Vermont home. During the 1850s and 1860s Morgans enjoyed increased popularity in the Midwest, upgrading stock in Ohio and becoming highly sought after as exhibition horses at State fairs. The most prolific breeder in the Midwest was Joseph C. Brunk of Rochester, Illinois, who introduced a breeding programme of great influence throughout the country. The Brunk foundation stock, of Vermont breeding, was purchased from the estate of Frank McGavock of Nashville, Tennessee, in 1893, comprising ten mares and a stallion, Chetco by Ben Franklin by Daniel Lambert. A later purchase was Jubilee de

Jubilee King (Penrod x Daisette), foaled June 1927. (*Photo courtesy AMHA*)

Flyhawk (Go Hawk x Florette), foaled August 1926, snoozing in the Western sun. (*Photo courtesy AMHA*)

Jarnette, son of the famous exhibition mare, Lady de Jarnette, and by Jubilee Lambert by Daniel Lambert.

J. C. Brunk bred a total of 267 foals from 1894 to 1934, breeding and purchasing many well-known sires and dams. He was a serious breeder and campaigner, travelling great distances to show, sell and purchase his stock. The show successes of the Brunk family abound. J. C. Brunk was a founding member of the Morgan Horse Club and was a Club director for 24 years. His family continued his breeding interests and actively contributed to the Club's development until relatively recently, mainly through his son J. Roy Brunk and his granddaughter Doris Ryan.

Some names seen in pedigrees which spell 'Brunk' breeding are Allen Franklin, Allen King, Go Hawk, Flyhawk, Tiffany, Congo, Penrod, Jubilee King, Juban, Red Vermont, Juzan and Agazizz.

'The hairy man from the east'

Robert Morgan states in his book *The Morgan Horse of the West* that Morgan horses were ridden by Wild Bill Hickock (1837–76) and Buffalo Bill Cody (1846–1917).

There is no doubt that during these times a horse was highly valued, being necessary for survival, hence horse stealing was punished with little mercy for the perpetrator. It is incredibly difficult to comprehend the distances which horses travelled and at what pace, not only for adventure, pioneering aims and war, but also to be sold. Buffalo Bill and his horses are highlighted in Robert Morgan's book. A half-bred Morgan called Charlie, belonging to Buffalo Bill, was so famous that he travelled overseas to Europe and in London was ridden by royalty.

Robert Morgan tells us:

> In London, the reporters said of Charlie, 'I saw Buffalo Bill's horse, Charlie, twenty years old. Mr Cody had ridden him upwards of fourteen years in all of his campaigns in the western exploits. This horse appeared at Windsor Castle, and when he died, Cody is reported to have said on the vessel SS *Persian Monarch*, "Old fellow, your journeys are over . . . Obedient to my call, gladly you bore your burden on, little knowing, little reckoning what the day might bring, shared sorrows and pleasures alike. Willing speed, tireless courage . . . you have never failed me. Ah, Charlie old fellow, I have had many friends, but few of whom I could say that . . . I loved you as you loved me. Men tell me that you have no soul; but if there is a heaven and scouts can enter there, I'll wait at the gate for you, old friend."'

Bill Cody was in the saddle from the time he was eight years old to the year of his death. He rode Morgans and part-bred Morgans many a time. He was a Pony Express rider, scout for the Seventh Kansas Cavalry, mustanger, buffalo hunter and Wild West Show presenter, and many of his best horses were acquired from the Indians. To catch the hardy Mustangs, Cody's horses had to be of superior calibre.

As increased numbers of adventurers, pioneers and homesteaders headed westward to claim their portion of the 276,000,000 acres opened up by the Homestead Act of 1862, Morgan horses went too in large numbers. The breed's proven endurance, soundness, cheerful and intelligent attitude, readiness for challenge and remarkable hauling capacity made it an ideal mount, pack and wagon horse to accompany those in their quest for new lands. Horses travelling often had to cover '40 miles a day carrying 200 pounds, living off whatever forage could be found along the way', encountering new and arduous terrain and conditions, resting with little shelter in extreme climates.

As the 'Red Man' faced the loss of his homelands and devastating spiritual injury,

Westward ho! Morgans love adventure and a change of scenery. (*Photo courtesy of AMHA*)

the white man plundered on, implementing changes such as the land and its native people had never known. Chief Luther Standing Bear of the Oglala band of Sioux was a teacher on the Rosebud Reservation in South Dakota and interpreter for Buffalo Bill's Wild West Show, which he joined in 1898. Later he spent his years lecturing and writing, and he wrote a passage that clearly explains the feelings of his people towards the land that must have felt the hoofprints of Morgan horses passing over it:

> We did not think of the great open plains, the beautiful rolling hills and the winding streams with tangled growth as 'wild'. Only to the white man was nature a 'wilderness' and only to him was the land 'infested' with 'wild' animals and 'savage' people. To us it was tame. Earth was bountiful and we were surrounded with blessings of the Great Mystery. Not until the hairy man from the east came and with brutal frenzy heaped injustices upon us and the families we loved was it 'wild' for us. When the very animals of the forest began fleeing from his approach, then it was for us that the 'Wild West' began.

Western Working Morgans

Morgan horses, respected for their contribution to other types and breeds, were soon recognized in their own right by a number of Western breeders. Gail Perlee of the Arizona Morgan Horse Association has done most of the research on Western Working Morgans, and published her findings in an article in the Arizona Morgan Horse Association magazine in 1991. She states:

> Actually Western Working Morgans have been around for as long as the other types, but have only been seen as a separate family for the last ten years. This has come about largely due to the research and writings of Lavonne Houlton of California. Western Working Morgans are not the product of one breeder, but rather are a group of related individuals developed specifically for cattle and ranch work in the rugged, wide open spaces of the American west. Today, although many of them still earn their oats as working cow horses, the family is used mostly as a source of size, substance, stamina and athletic ability within the breed.

Quite a number of the sires and dams and lines stemming from them throughout this chapter are to be found in British Morgan pedigrees.

Texas

By the 1880s Texas had contributed to the restriction of movement of the Indian people by laying railroad tracks spanning the vast areas of the state. One of the new settlers of the late 1880s was Richard Sellman, who with his family left the southeastern state of Maryland to lay claim to 40,000 acres of land near Rochelle, naming his territory Mountain Vale Ranch. He was described as extremely wealthy, upright and a true philanthropist, and was highly praised for distributing his Morgans at his own expense to benefit other breeding and training programmes. Sellman purchased his first stallion, Major Gordon, a 16-hand black horse weighing over 1,260 pounds, in 1886. Between 1886 and 1879 Sellman bred over 20 broodmares by Major Gordon.

Sellman wished to stay true to Morgan lines, repudiating actions of other breeders who utilized Morgans purely for cross-breeding. He used quite a number of stallions but perhaps the most influential was Headlight Morgan (Ethan Allen 2nd x Lady Stratton), indubitably an outstanding stallion, bred in Illinois and foaled in Kansas in 1893.

Headlight Morgan arrived at the Sellman Ranch at the age of 21 and lived another twelve years, siring 112 foals for Sellman from 1915 to 1921. He was highly acclaimed, being given the title 'King of Morgans'.

By the time of his death in 1925, Sellman had registered an incredible 689 Morgans, becoming one of the largest breeders in Morgan history. Unfortunately many of the Morgans sold by the Sellman estate were lost to the breed because registration papers were not transferred.

Also interesting is that many of the descendants of the Sellman herd were later registered as Quarter Horses, a compliment to Sellman's desire to retain the breed's qualities of durability, although not in line with his feelings against cross-breeding the Morgan.

California

Sellman stock became the foundation stock of a number of breeding programmes in California. Reginald O. Parsons of the Montcrest Ranch, not far from the Oregon border, purchased a group of Sellman mares and a Headlight stallion in 1920. Montcrest Sellman (Joe Baily x Kitty B) from Parson's first foal crop was sold in 1932 to the millionaire newspaper magnate, Randolf Hearst, to head his own stud at the Piedmont Land and Cattle Co., siring stallions Montabelle and Redman. Morgans were also bred at Hearst's Sunical ranch.

Roland Hill, owner of the Horseshoe Land and Cattle Co. of California and the Blue Horse Ranch in Nevada, both of enormous acreage, began breeding Morgans in 1922. His endeavours to breed ideal ranch horses using various breed and type crosses having failed, Hill purchased Redwood Morgan (Headlight Morgan x Bonnie A by Major Antoine) from Sellman. So impressed was he with Redwood, Hill personally selected 13 broodmares from Sellman's herd, adding a further 14 in 1924.

Deeming Redwood too closely bred to the mares, Hill sold him in 1923, purchasing instead Pat Allen (Allen King x Patrona) from J. C. Brunk. Pat Allen was later replaced by the Government stallion Querido and his daughters were bred to the Government stallion Sonfield (Mansfield x Quietude by Troubadour of Willowmoor) to fulfil Hill's breeding programme.

Hill, another prolific Morgan breeder, registered nearly 300 mares, and their descendants were widely distributed throughout the state. An example of Hill's breeding bringing us up to the present day is Helen Mala (Querido x Hemala by Headlight Morgan). She produced the full sisters, Helen May and Helen Field, both by Sonfield. Helen May was the dam of Kennebec Count, three times US Combined Driving Pairs Champion with his son Kennebec Russel, the first Morgan horses to serve on the US Equestrian Team in Europe.

According to Gail Perlee:

In 1940 the last major sire was brought into the California branch of the Western Working family when the Davis breeding farm purchased the Brunk stallion Red Vermont (Jubilee King x Daisy Knox). Some of his breeding sons were Monty Vermont, Domino Vermont, Easter Vermont, Sireson (who went to the Neelys in Idaho) and Homestake.

Two of his best-known daughters were Verdonna Vermont (dam of a series of show champions by the Lippitt stallion Moro Hill Gay Ethan) and Ginger Vermont, dam of Monty Vermont. Today most Western Working Morgans trace to California stock several times.

Kennebec Count and Kennebec Russel of the Kennebec Morgan Horse Farm, Maine, owned by Margaret Gardiner. Myopia National Championships 1985, Larry Poulin whip. (*Photo courtesy Margaret Gardiner*)

Kansas

One of the most significant horses to be used in Kansas was Linsley (General Gates x Sunflower Maid by Headlight Morgan). In fact his dam had been bred in Kansas but was purchased as a yearling by the Government Farm in 1911, foaling Linsley in 1918. Linsley, a 'strapping' 15.2 hand, red chestnut stallion, sired 53 registered foals for Elmer Brown of Halstead, Kansas, after arriving at the Brown ranch in 1921. Brown's broodmare band shouted good 'old' breeding, including three daughters of Headlight Morgan. Out of numerous breedings, 119 registered by Brown, came many useful sires and dams, several of which were distributed to other successful breeding programmes.

One of the best Linsley sons was Chocolate (out of Lady Spar by Spar Hawk). He spent his later years with R. S. Sentney who described him as 'the best cow horse I ever rode. He can turn on a dime and cut fish right out of the pond.' For George Hineman he sired Powerful, a stallion used by the Pine Ridge Indian Agency in South Dakota and later by O. E. Sutter, producing stock for the Dot S Morgans. For R. S. Sentney Chocolate sired Raymond S. Sentney out of a mare solidly linebred to Headlight Morgan. This stallion contributed to the Thies Ranch breeding programme of Dodge City, and many of his daughters were amongst a consignment of the famous Thies mares purchased by Cecil Ferguson for use in the Broadwall breeding programme in Rhode Island. The best-known horse to be bred by the Fergusons was the 15.1 hand chestnut stallion Parade. His dam Mansphyllis, by the Government bred stallion Mansfield, was out of the well-bred Western mare Paragraph, by Jubilee King. Parade's sire, Cornwallis, traced to Justin Morgan in eight generations and is registered in the Lippitt Register. During his 31 years of life Parade was an influential sire and won championships in-hand, in harness (both pairs and singles) and under saddle. His ability to master a high standard of dressage training resulted in him joining the Spanish Riding School of Vienna's Lippizan stallions on tour of the United States in 1964, at the invitation of Colonel Alois Podhajsky. Parade's son Broadwall Drum Major also performed with the School.

Some of Linsley's most influential sons were Chocolate, Linspar, Sparbeau, Sir Linsley, Rosco Morgan and Hawk Jim. Linspar, foaled in 1925, was used by the L.U. Sheep Co. in Wyoming. Sparbeau, full brother to Linspar, went to Roland Hill in California. Hawk Jim, full brother to Chocolate and foaled in 1929, went to the US Army Remount Service, in later years standing at Merle Evan's Crabapple Farm in Ohio, where he sired the versatile stallion Devon Hawk.

Parade (Cornwallis x Mansphyllis) and Colonel Podhajsky, director of the Spanish Riding School, Vienna. Note Parade's excellent bone, musculature, and expression of character. (*Photo courtesy Meg Ferguson*)

Other lines containing the blood of Linsley are Beamington, Waseeka's Nocturne, Plains King and of course Raymond S. Sentney.

Montana and Wyoming

At the dispersal of the Sellman estate of over 300 Morgans, the US Department of Agriculture bought 17 mares and shipped them to the US Range Livestock Experiment Station at Miles City, Montana. The mares, when bred to the Government stallions Revere (Mansfield x Folly) and Monterey (Mansfield x

Scotanna), became the heart of a breeding programme producing 82 registered Morgans between 1925 and 1934. When the Station was closed the horses went to various ranchers and also Indian Agencies in Montana, Nevada, Wyoming and Washington.

In 1925 the Jacksons of Montana, breeders of cross-bred Morgans, purchased their first registered Morgan stock. They used the stallions Chief Bugler (Tyee x Gala Girl), Monte L (Major R.M. x Jumina by Jubilee King), Fleetfield (Mentor x Norma by Canfield), Ken Carmen (Jubilee King x Heroda), Rosefield (Sonfield x Rose Mala by Querido) and Senatefield (Fleetfield x Parka), a homebred stallion.

The L.U. Sheep Co. of Worland, Wyoming purchased the famous Flyhawk (Go Hawk x Florette) from the J. C. Brunk herd of Illinois. He became a top cow horse, siring so many offspring that he had to be sold to the Padlock Ranch near by. In 1939 Helen Brunk Greenwalt traded King de Jarnette for Flyhawk, bringing him home to the east. He became Champion Morgan Stallion at the Illinois State Fair in 1940 and 1941. In the early 1940s the L.U. Sheep Co. acquired another Brunk stallion, Senator Graham (Senator Knox x Fanita by Tiffany), who when bred to Flyhawk daughters produced excellent ranch horses, one, Starfire (x Wanda), being the sire of Waseeka's Nocturne. Starfire was sold to Upwey Farm in 1950, and later to a Colonel Emerson. He only sired nine foals altogether.

The Northwest

Morgans have apparently been in the Northwest since the 1850s. John Clise of Willowmoor Morgans, Washington, began his breeding programme in 1906 with mares from New England and the stallion Troubador (Jubilee de Jarnette x Bird Pepper). Troubador was bred by C. X. Laribee of Home Park, Montana. His best-known son was Troubador of Willowmoor (out of Fannie 2nd by Bob Morgan), purchased with other stock from the Clise ranch in 1911 by the Government Farm. Sonfield, whose dam Quietude was by Troubadour of Willowmoor, stood at stud with Leo Beckly of Beckridge Morgans at Mt Vernon, Washington state.

Clarence Shaw of Walla Walla, Washington was the largest Western Working Morgan breeder of the Northwest, producing over 400 Morgans. The Shawalla programme was founded in 1954 using the 'good roping, pick up and bulldogging horse, Silver Rockwood (Agazizz x May Rockwood by Rockwood) as his foundation sire'. Silver Rockwood was foaled in 1942, bred by Robert Tynan of Stella, Nebraska. His sire Agazizz was a Brunk grandson of Jubilee King and his dam, May Rockwood,

Troubador of Willowmoor posing in front of the statue of Justin Morgan at the unveiling ceremony, Middlebury, Vermont, 1 October 1921. (*Photo courtesy AMHA*)

Quietude (Troubador of Willowmoor x Ruth), the dam of Sonfield and Upwey Ben Don, with colt foal Damascus. (*Photo courtesy AMHA*)

was by a Government stallion out of a Headlight Morgan mare, showing the continued demand for Brunk and Sellman stock. Shaw went to Roland Hill for his broodmares. Phil Morrison of Grants Pass, Oregon, founded his breeding programme with the Hearst-bred Sonoma (Piedmont Apache x Rose B by Querido), foaled in 1938. Morrison is remembered for one of his best mares, Abbonette, a daughter of the Remount stallion Abbott (Monterey x Klyona) which was brought in from California.

Utah

According to Gail Perlee:

> In Utah three stallions stand out as Western Working sires. The first of these was Stellar (Mentor x Naiad). Bred by the US Government Farm, he was foaled in

1948 and sold to J. Holman Waters of Salt Lake City in 1951 when the Government stock was dispersed. For Mel Frandsen of Mary-Mels Morgans at American Fork, he crossed well with Brunk mares to found a line of quality using ranch horses. Out of the great mare Wingo (Flying Jubilee x Cynthia) he got the full brothers Omar Shariff and Gringo, who went on to found dynasties of their own.

Second to arrive was Flying Jubilee (Flyhawk x Jumina by Jubilee King). Also foaled in 1948 and bred by Helen Brunk Greenwalt, he stood for two years at the L.U. Sheep Co. before being sold to Cowboy writer Ern Pedler in 1953. Pedler used the stud hard for mustanging over the roughest terrain imaginable, and of course for breeding as well. His daughters, especially those out of Brunk or Western Working mares, were wonderful producers.

Last to arrive, in 1957, was the great broodmare sire Townshend Gaymeade (Meade x Gayselba by Ulysses). Foaled in 1949 on the farm of Anna Ela, he was purchased in 1953 by Helen Brunk Greenwalt and transferred to the L.U. Sheep Co. There he ran with a band of mares until sold to Ern Pedler in 1957. Pedler kept him for only one year before selling him to Tas-Tee Farm in Ohio. Gaymeade left excellent daughters in Wyoming, Utah and the Mid-West including Ecstasy (dam of Bill Bailey), Osogay (foundation mare for Paramount), Belle Meade (foundation mare for Dick Nelson Primavera stock horses), Gay Maid of Wenloch, Rosemeade and Gay Flower.

5 The characteristics and contribution of the Morgan horse

Present-day requirements

The Morgan temperament is the most fundamental requirement of the breed today. Besides tractability, intelligence and an endearing sense of humour, the Morgan possesses a unique keenness to accomplish all that is required of it to the best of its ability. This resounding cheerfulness and generosity makes the Morgan easy to train, safe, reliable and enthusiastic. It is this temperament which has caused individuals in the breed to be both versatile and capable of specialization to a high standard. No matter what other characteristics may have changed within the breed, this precious attribute has remained remarkably consistent.

However, the prospective novice Morgan owner should note that this intelligence and quickness to learn does not mean that any less attention should be paid to training than with any other breed or type of horse. To quote the apt words of an old friend, Derek Courian: 'You can easily teach your Morgan everything you don't want it to know.' Another factor relating to breed keenness and learning ability is that many Morgans have that challenging predisposition to anticipate what may be required. From a humorous point of view this is handy if you are following directional arrows during an FEI driving event and suffer from short-sightedness, but is more of a challenge, perhaps, if executing a complicated ridden dressage test.

Morgan tractability is thus not absolute docility but is a willingness to comply even in an energetic or excited state. This type of expression of character, for example, is often demonstrated by the Morgan show horse, particularly in in-hand and Park classes and some Pleasure classes. Breeding programmes have developed over the years which strive for specific ability and expression of character to suit the various competitive and pleasure uses of the breed. Whilst each animal should be assessed on its individual merit prior to purchase, some advantage can be gained by studying the breeding of a Morgan to assess its likely qualities.

Conformation requirements vary as the Morgan faces increased competition both within and outside the breed in a huge assortment of specialized skills. However, to excel in any sphere much attention needs to be paid to correct, strong and sound con-

63

formation and a natural freedom of movement. The majority of breeders realize this. There is little doubt that those special Morgan characteristics of yesteryear are still very necessary in the breed today.

The Morgan Horse Association Judging Standards as adopted by the AMHA Inc. list a large and comprehensive assortment of conformational faults to guide judges and breeders in their quest to maintain a high standard of breed type and conformation. Conformation faults existing within the Morgan breed are really no different to those of other breeds. However, some to look out for are boxy feet, a tendency to stand base narrow or wide, pigeon or splayed toes, weak stifles, a hollow (dippy) back and too much refinement resulting in a lack of muscular substance and bone.

The strong emphasis on the Morgan horse as a performance and competition animal has tended to increase the demand for taller Morgans, up to 16 hands or 16.2 hands, with an average requirement in the range 15 hands to 15.2 hands. Understandably, concern and disputes over changes within the breed still surface today, with regard to loss of breed type, conformation, way of going and possibly the renowned Morgan versatility as a consequence.

As a versatile individual, however, there is no evidence to suggest that the Morgan is losing ground. In fact the opposite is the case and this special attribute of the breed seems to be increasingly important. At one time breed versatility in general received less promotion than it does now. Extensive advertising of the Morgan as a show horse overshadowed promotion of its other uses. What has changed (and I think this often causes confusion) is the expectation of what versatility is.

The competitive market, whether in breed or open competition, glorifies those who attain the highest goals but who, in fairness, represent a minority group. Higher standards at the top end of the competitive market mean that specialization is necessary for success, and the pleasure and utility value and the average all-round competitive importance of the Morgan is therefore overlooked. But it is still there, as it actually caters for the majority of Morgan owners. If to be recognized as versatile the individual Morgan has to attain the top standard in a collection of pursuits, then this becomes a very tall order for both horses and people.

The individual, versatile Morgan is found in abundance worldwide, the heart and flag-bearer of the breed. He can be the ideal family, 4H and Pony Club horse, the working horse, the therapeutic programme and community horse, as well as taking his place in competitive events for junior and senior, amateur and professional. The beauty of owning a Morgan is that you know you have a horse that can do many things and can change interests and activities with you. In short, the temperament of the Morgan combined with its characteristic strength and durability enable it to adapt to any requirement, attaining the best standards possible in the circumstances.

The breed standard of perfection

The standard given below is from the American Morgan Horse Association Inc. (AMHA) Judging Standards for in-hand classes and any other classes where the rules indicate that breed type and conformation are to be considered.

A. Type is the ideal or standard of perfection for the breed. A Morgan is distinctive for its stamina and vigor, personality and eagerness and strong natural way of moving.

B. Conformation is the degree of perfection of the component parts and their relationship to each other.

1.   The head should be expressive with broad forehead, large prominent eyes, with straight or slightly dished, short face, firm fine lips, large nostrils and well rounded jowls. The ears should be short and shapely, set rather wide apart and carried alertly. Mares may have a slightly longer ear.

2.   The throatlatch is slightly deeper than other breeds and should be refined sufficiently to allow proper flexion at the poll and normal respiration.

3.   The neck should come out on top of the withers of an extremely well angulated shoulder with depth from the top of the withers to point of shoulder. It should be relatively fine in relation to sex. It should be slightly arched and should blend with the withers and back. The top line of the neck should be considerably longer than the bottom line. The stallion should have more crest than the mare or gelding.

4.   The wither should be well defined and extend into the back in proportion to the angulation of the shoulder.

5.   The body should be compact with a short back, close coupling, broad loins, deep flank, well sprung ribs, croup long and well muscled with tail attached high, carried gracefully and straight.

6.   The stifle should be placed well forward and low in the flank area.

7.   The leg should be straight and sound with short cannons, flat bone, and an appearance of overall substance with refinement. The forearm should be relatively long in proportion to the cannon. The pasterns should have sufficient length and angulation to provide a light springy step.

8. The feet should be in proportion to the size of the horse, round, open at the heel, with concave sole and hoof of dense structure.

9. Viewed from the front, the chest should be well developed. The front legs should be perpendicular to the ground and closely attached to the body.

10. Viewed from the side, the top line represents a gentle curve from the poll to the back, giving the impression of the neck sitting on top of the withers rather than in front of them, continuing to a short, straight back and a relatively level croup rounding into a well muscled thigh. The tail should be attached high and carried well arched. At maturity the croup should not be higher than the withers. The underline should be long and the body deep through the heart girth and flanks. The extreme angulation of the shoulder results in the arm being a little more vertical than other breeds, placing the front legs slightly further forward on the body. The front legs should be straight and perpendicular to the ground. The rear cannons should be perpendicular to the ground when points of hocks and buttocks are in the same vertical lines.

11. Viewed from the rear, the croup should be well rounded, thighs and gaskins well muscled. Legs should be straight. The gaskins should be relatively long in relation to the cannon.

12. The height ranges from 14.1 to 15.2, with some individuals under or over.

13. Horses must be serviceably sound – i.e. must not show evidence of lameness, broken wind or complete loss of sight in either eye.

14. Stallions two years old and over must have all the fully developed characteristics of a stallion. Mature stallions must be masculine in appearance. Mares must be feminine in appearance.

C. Other distinctive attributes of the Morgan horse are his presence and personality. These include:

1. Animation
2. Stamina
3. Vigor
4. Alertness
5. Adaptability
6. Attitude
7. Tractability

A complete set of judging guidelines for all Morgan Horse Divisions, *The Morgan Horse Judging Standards*, is available from AMHA Headquarters, Shelburne,

Vermont, USA. The British Morgan Horse Society (BMHS) have adopted the AMHA Breed and Judging Standards with a few additions and alterations, and these are obtainable from the BMHS headquarters in England.

Since 1947, despite the efforts and concerns of quite a number of individuals to retain the 'strong' and 'powerful' description of the breed since the early 1900s, changes have been made to the 'Standard of Perfection' in favour of refinement. These changes have related to Morgan neck descriptions, varying from 'deeply crested' to 'well crested' to 'slightly crested' and finally to the present description of 'relatively fine'. Obviously refinements of this nature have not only affected the neck development of Morgans within certain breeding programmes, particularly those aimed at the show ring and specific competitions, but have also affected the whole individual. Thus a portion of the Morgan population exhibits less overall muscular substance and has lost the 'strong' and 'powerful' look as originally defined.

This desire to refine certain characteristics is not unique to Morgan breeders. It is widely thought that many breeds have reached their limits of refinement, and that if refinement continues irrationally the breed will lose the type and attributes which took so long to evolve and which will eventually become less distinguishable.

The height range of the Morgan has also undergone changes, originally being 14.1 to 15.1 hands, then 14.2 to 15.2 hands, and finally compromising on the present range of 14.1 to 15.2 hands with some over or under.

Besides the 'Standard of Perfection' – the ultimate guide for breeders, purchasers, judges and the competitive showing fraternity – there are no mandatory avenues of inspection and evaluation (e.g. licensing or grading schemes) available specifically for the Morgan breed, although inspection and evaluation tests are presently being organized by the Morgan International Sport Horse Record (MISHR) in association with other recognized breed authorities related to performances. Therefore, at this time, the potential for refining and significantly changing the breed remains in the hands of breeders, often under the influence of judges and new trends.

The Morgan contribution to other breeds

Stamina, endurance, soundness, an abundance of muscle and good strong conformation, combined with a steady and tractable temperament, intelligence and wit were many of the characteristics required for the successful development of other American breeds and types. These attributes are clearly still in demand today for the breeding of quality and capable horses and ponies.

It is widely accepted that the Thoroughbred played a major part in the overall development of light horse breeds in America. However, the Morgan came a close second, passing on traits that culminated in the successful development of useful performance animals.

The American Saddlebred

A very large percentage of all Saddlebreds carry Morgan blood, mainly through Cabell's Lexington, Blood's Black Hawk, Blood Chief, the famous Indian Chief, who was registered in the American Saddle Horse Register (ASHR), and Telegraph. Joseph Battell attested that the stallions selected as foundation sires by the National Saddle Horse Breeders Association in 1899 were largely of Morgan descent, and in fact there are 714 entries with direct male lines to the original Justin Morgan sire listed amongst the 11,997 horses registered in Volumes I to IV of the Saddle Horse Register.

The American Saddlebred derives his size and fineness predominantly from the Thoroughbred, his fluent gaits from early Colonial pacing stock, and his animated action, substance and stamina from Morgan blood.

The American Standardbred Horse

The American trotting horse largely evolved from Morgan blood in the nineteenth century. So intense was the fervour for consistently improved trotters that newer and faster lines developed which surpassed the abilities of the Morgans. However, it was well recognized that infusions of Morgan blood to this 'new' trotting stock contributed increased stamina and substance and a purity to the Standardbred trotting gait. Because of constant outcrossing and neglect of the continuation of pure Morgan family lines the development of the Standardbred became the foremost threat to the perpetuation of the Morgan as a breed.

In fact the trotters were so popular that Shepard F. Knapp 3320, bred by George Snell of Turner, Maine, and foaled in 1857 (registered in the American Trotting Registry, No. 282, Vol. IV), was shipped to Europe in 1864. He was sired by the Eaton horse and was a descendant of Sherman Morgan. He was exhibited in Paris and bought by Major Stapylton, a Yorkshire landowner. Major Stapylton travelled the horse in Yorkshire and East Anglia.

Shepard F. Knapp was one of the most celebrated trotters of his time and the sire of many successful Hackneys and trotters in Britain, such as Washington (who in turn sired the acclaimed high-stepping show mare, Movement), Rapid Road, Norfolk Shepherd and Primrose, one of the treasured mares of the Brookfield Stud owned by the MP, William Burdett-Coutts. Primrose was the dam of Rising Star and Rising Star of the East.

On 10 May 1947 Dr C. Parkes, recognized as one of the foremost authorities on the Morgan, spoke to a gathering of New England Morgan Horse breeders in Boston on 'The Morgan of Distinction'. His speech was later reprinted in *Cavalcade of American Horses* by Pers Crowell. Speaking about the early development of the road horse Dr Parkes said:

> Going back to about 1850, when the intensification of the blood horse began, a horse with speed was a very valuable animal. The horse was the only means of transportation: roads were improved and harness racing was a favorite sport. The Morgan up to this time and for a few more years was the fastest available harness horse. Black Hawk 20, a grandson of Justin Morgan, and Ethan Allen 50, a great grandson, were the champion trotting stallions of their day.
>
> Hambletonian 10 was foaled in 1849 and produced, during his twenty-six years of life, 1,321 offspring. The offspring of this horse mixed with the fast Morgans of the next few years produced the Standardbred, which was faster and more popular as a harness horse than the true Morgan. Several families of Morgans were absorbed in this way and forgotten. The Morril family is a good example of this.

The Tennessee Walker

Allan F-1, foaled in 1886, was the number one foundation sire of the Tennessee Walking Horse, and a horse of Morgan descent. He was by Allandorf, by Onward, by George Wilkes, who had Morgan blood through his dam, Dolly Spanker. Allan F-1 was out of Maggie Marshall, who was by Bradford's Telegraph by Black Hawk, and therefore traced directly to Justin Morgan through Sherman Morgan in the top line of her pedigree.

Roan Allan F-38, a son of Allan F-1, traced back to the Gifford Morgan through his dam's sire, adding further infusions of Morgan blood. Twenty-five of the breed's top stallions in 1949 traced in direct male line to Roan Allan.

Two other foundation sires claimed to be of Morgan breeding, yet with 'No record of pedigree' in the American Saddle Horse Registry, are Old Imported Copperbottom (Canadian) and Old Tom Hal (Canadian). Pers Crowell thought it extremely unlikely that such multiple gaited horses as these two could have come from a preponderance of Morgan blood, yet Old Tom Hal was registered by Battell in the Morgan Register as a pacer (No. 31), if indeed this is one and the same horse, sired in Canada by either Justin Morgan or a son of his! Copperbottom is also registered as No. 66. Pers Crowell wrote:

> If the two old-time sires Tom Hal and Copperbottom could be positively traced to Justin Morgan, it would indeed add even greater glory to the Morgan breed as a progenitor of great horses.
>
> In checking through the list of foundation stock in the Tennessee Walking Horse Register, it is extremely difficult to find pedigrees that are not sprinkled profusely with Morgan, through the Black Hawk strain, or the Copperbottoms or the Tom Hals.

The American Quarter Horse

Many people have likened the qualities of the Quarter Horse to those of the Morgan. This is no wonder because both breeds, known for their stamina, endurance and intelligence, initially developed from the horses of east coast America. They also share a common ancestor, the influential Godolphin Arabian. From there Quarter Horse development was influenced by Spanish horse blood, as opposed to the trotting horse influence of the Morgan.

However, both breeds possessed the necessary qualities to enable them to complete the arduous journeys and tasks of the legendary West and were perpetuated for their hardiness and ability to do the work required rather than for pedigree. Quarter Horses were not registered until as late as 1940 and even though we are aware that quite a number of the Morgans dispersed from the Sellman herd in Texas were later registered as Quarter Horses, heavy in the blood of Headlight Morgan, there are no accurate records to estimate the Morgan's influence on the breed.

Military Morgans

Morgan horses are well remembered for their military service around the world.

Their help was enlisted during the Mexican War, the American Civil War and World War I, where their talents as cavalry mounts were converted to artillery, ambulance hauling and pack use, due to the trench warfare tactics of the enemy. During World War I Morgans numbered amongst millions of American horses in action, leading to huge losses and casualties. Exhaustion was a major factor as horses had to negotiate deeply rutted, muddy roads and tracks, usually weighted to capacity.

Magellan, a stallion bred by the US Government Farm, was one of 26 horses exported to Nationalist China in 1947 for the purpose of improving cavalry stock. He was reported to have been sighted during the Korean War being ridden by a Chinese Communist General!

Though there have been many Morgans remembered for their military contribution, one of the most eulogized and famous military Morgans was the gelding, Rienzi. He was the charger of General Phillip Sheridan, the most exemplary Northern Cavalry officer of the American Civil War. Sheridan is said never to have ridden any other horse during his campaign, from the time it was presented to him by an officer of the 2nd Michigan Cavalry soon after he took command of the regiment whilst stationed at Rienzi, Mississippi, on 25 May 1862.

'Sheridan's ride' on Rienzi, the Morgan charger. (*Photo courtesy AMHA*)

A description of Rienzi is given in the memoirs of General Sheridan:

> He was of Morgan stock and about three years old. He was jet black excepting three white feet, sixteen hands high and strongly built with great powers of endurance . . . He was an animal of great intelligence and immense strength . . . He always held his head high and by the quickness of his movements gave many persons the idea that he was exceedingly impetuous and fiery. This was not so, for he could at any time be controlled by a firm hand and a few words and he was as cool and quiet under fire as an old soldier.

Rienzi, ridden in many battles and wounded on occasion, survived the war and lived to be 19, 'attended to the last with all the care due the faithful service he had rendered'. His hide was stuffed and placed on exhibit in the Smithsonian Institute.

Early exports

The Morgan contribution to other strains of horses has spread outside the confines of North America. Exportations were made from as early as the 1850s, during the times of increased popularity of the fast trotter. Many of these horses were shipped to Europe.

From the early 1900s many fine mares and stallions were exported worldwide, sold by private breeders and owners and also by the US Government Farm and the US Department of Agriculture, working together with the Remount Service breeding and training programmes.

Examples of countries purchasing Morgans for stock improvement and military use from 1912 include Puerto Rico; Japan, which purchased 11 Morgans for the Emperor's stud in 1920; Brazil; the Republic of El Salvador, Central America; Cuba, whose Army Remount Service purchased Morgans in 1931 and several mares in 1933; Trinidad; Hawaii, which first purchased the stallion Querido in 1937, and after gradually increasing the stock added a further group purchase of approximately 17 Morgans, mainly mares, in 1951.

World War II temporarily limited the export of Morgans. However, in 1947 the Chinese Ministry of Defence purchased 26 Morgans from an assortment of individual breeders. Today, as we shall see, Morgans have been exported worldwide.

6 The Morgan in America today

The American Morgan Horse Association Inc.

The American Morgan Horse Association Inc. (AMHA) describes itself as:

> A broadly based international membership organization rendering important services to the entire Morgan horse world. Its exclusive responsibility is the day to day operation of the registry, breed related services and breed promotions.

The AMHA has experienced rapid growth and development, especially since the 1960s, and in the 1990s represents the interests of a junior and senior membership of approximately 12,000, a huge contrast when compared with 1927 when there were fewer than 40 members. There are about 96 associated National Clubs, which include 34 Youth Breed Clubs, divided into nine regions, each region represented by one or two AMHA Directors. Each region holds numerous associated breed shows and events and its own Regional Championship, and the annual Grand National and World Championship Morgan Horse Show is held in Oklahoma City, Oklahoma. This show is held over seven days and includes every assortment of discipline imaginable, creating over 400 individual classes.

There are presently 11 recognized Morgan national service organizations which support specific interests and activities. Internationally recognized breed clubs are listed in Canada, Great Britain (these two countries also maintain International Registries which have reciprocity with the AMHA), Sweden, Germany, Italy, Australia and New Zealand.

The AMHA plays a very supportive role, in particular encouraging young people to involve themselves with the breed. The American Morgan Horse Association Youth (AMHAY) is an international organization open to all young people under the age of 22 years, interested in any aspect of the breed. Youth membership spans the United States, Canada, Great Britain and Sweden. Many educational and recreational activities and programmes are organized for Youth members plus various scholarships and awards. One of these is the AMHA Youth of the Year Contest, the successful entrant winning a month-long trip, usually abroad, as an ambassador for the AMHAY. Junior riders in all parts of Canada and the United States compete at local and regional shows to win AMHAY Silver Medals, hoping to qualify for the Gold Medal finals held at the Grand National and World Championships.

The Registry

The population of Morgan horses alive today in the USA is estimated at approximately 80,000. To add further safeguard to the Rules of Registration, blood typing has been researched and used in part for some time, the rules before 1991 requiring it for 'maiden mares, mares bred via semen transport, donor dams when embryo transfer is done, all stallions siring foals, and mares who are bred twice within a 35-day period.'

At the 1991 AMHA Convention, the AMHA Board of Directors unanimously approved new Registry Rules and Regulations, one of the most important being:

> Effective January 1st, 1992, every Morgan horse who is presented for registration will be required to have its blood type on file.

The Magazine

The first breed magazine appeared on 15 October 1941, *The Morgan Horse News Bulletin*, issued and financed by Owen Moon Jr, a director and president of the Morgan Horse Club Inc., avid Morgan breeder, show organizer and participant. Upon his death in 1947 his wife donated the magazine to the Morgan Horse Club Inc.

The magazine has grown from a twelve-page publication to a mammoth glossy and colourful monthly magazine, *The Morgan Horse*, often totalling over 340 pages. It provides extensive feature coverage concerning the Morgan breed, past and present, profiles of people and horses, training and general horse care, regional and international activities, programmes and news. Today all aspects of the breed in competition are highlighted via articles and impressive advertising, portraying the Morgan's versatility and development very clearly to the readership. Columns are also extremely informative, ranging from readership letters, reviews, relevant information and updates concerning the American Morgan Horse Association and the Registry and much more. It is probably one of the outstanding equine publications produced today, always searching to improve, and available through subscription worldwide, with postage overseas usually more than the subscription costs.

Showing

Showing in twentieth-century North America is a far cry from the parades, fairs and expositions of the nineteenth century. There is a comprehensive national network of shows of various descriptions, run under the governing influence of the American Horse Shows Association. Horses and exhibitors are becoming increasingly competitive and specialized.

Over the last 40 years AMHA shows have witnessed their most significant changes. The showing of Morgans was greatly affected by the commercial development of the specialized Morgan show horse, creating new interest, recognition and business both for the breed and the AMHA. With the advent of the professional horseman (and as a result the introduction of amateur divisions) and concentrated promotion, a new body of people was drawn to the breed purely as a show horse prospect. Many breeding and professional training programmes evolved to suit the new demands, developing specific characteristics and abilities in the Morgan to accommodate modern-day requirements and trends.

Trainers faced increased pressures from this new class of owner to produce winning horses in the shortest possible time. Various controversies arose regarding the use of gadgetry and shoeing techniques (length of foot and weight of shoe) to enhance or perfect performance, especially that of the high-stepping Park Morgan. By 1959 rules had to be introduced to prevent abuse, and have been reviewed and revised at intervals since.

The horse show is the showcase of every breed. In the Morgan world, great emphasis is placed on immaculate presentation and the enhancement of the breed's most noticeable features, as well as the physical and mental conditioning required for the performance at hand. When prepared for a show the Morgan should be in good condition, in good weight but not over fat. He should be fit for his performance requirement, his muscles well toned and firm. He should also have a full mane and tail, well brushed and picked out. For that special finished appearance the inside and outer edges of the ears, the hairs over the eyes, on the muzzle and under the lower jaw are trimmed. From just behind the ears a bridle path is trimmed, usually two to six inches along the top of the crest to highlight the line of the neck and throat. In the case of the Morgans performing in breed Hunter classes (English tack and attire) often only the immediate bridle path is trimmed and the mane and the tail plaited, though there is no discrimination against horses who exhibit with full mane and tail. Any long hairs on the lower legs are also removed.

Showing in-hand is probably the least stressful activity for new exhibitors, offering them a chance to familiarize themselves (especially at small local shows) with the importance of show presentation, the behaviour and manners of their horses and their overall performance. In North America and in Britain special Showmanship classes are provided for youth and novice exhibitors, judged purely on the showing technique of the handler. This type of introductory class takes the sting out of those first-time nerves.

Showing in-hand can also be beneficial to the young horse, as he too can familiarize himself with the distractions and excitement of a show whilst being asked to stand still or perform with reasonable decorum in response to his handler's requests and expectations.

Exhibitors of in-hand stock should wear well-fitting, conservative clothes which add to their overall presentation and the decorum of the show ring, and do not impair their ability to trot their horses up in hand. Fitness of the handler is recommended too!

According to the AMHA Judging Standards, effective January 1993, which are also adopted by other Morgan breed organizations around the world, Appointments (i.e. tack) for in-hand classes are as follows:

1. Weanlings are shown in halters and must be barefooted.
2. Yearlings may be shown in halters or appropriate bridles and must be barefooted.
3. The use of the appropriate bridle with a snaffle, curb or stallion bit is recommended for all others. A show halter is acceptable.

Special show halters can be purchased, some with thin coloured browbands and nosebands. Stallions three years and over should wear a bridle with either a stallion or curb bit to facilitate maximum control and safety. However, it is advised that the use of curb bits in the young horse be avoided, especially in novice hands, as the potentially strong action of this type of bit could cause problems if mismanaged. It is strongly advised that horses to be shown in curb bits are well accustomed to them prior to showing.

In-hand classes are very much the breeder's division. Quality, conformation, temperament and close adherence to breed type are all judged, along with the horse's way of going at walk and trot. The performance of the in-hand Morgan is not too dissimilar to that of the Hackney and Welsh Cob in Britain, in that a degree of individual presence (attitude) and exuberant expression at the trot is sought, as well as show

76

stance, often the deciding factor for the judge. The show stance of the Morgan, described as 'parking out' or the 'parked out' position, is when the front legs of the horse are perpendicular to the ground and his hind legs are stretched out behind. Horses are exhibited showing different degrees of stretch, some extreme and unappealing which look very unnatural and uncomfortable. Judges are recommended to ask the exhibitor to move the hind legs up under the horse for inspection, mainly because a hollow back may be the reason for the horse being excessively stretched out. By having the horse parked out his croup is lowered, resulting in the back looking more level, as is the fashion. Also the horse's shoulders are accentuated and he is able to place his neck in a more upright position and hold his head high in the ultimate pose. This stance is said to have developed during English carriage days, as it meant that the horse could not move off quickly, making it safer for passengers stepping in and out of carriages. This stance was later adopted for the Saddlebred horse, and since Saddlebreds and Morgans competed against one another during the leisure boom after World War II, Morgans, whose numbers were not enough to warrant their own divisions at shows, adopted the stance to compete against Saddlebreds.

Show divisions which were avidly promoted during the peak years of the Morgan show horse are the Park and Pleasure Morgan classes, both ridden and driven (an aspect of the breed which has been adopted as the basis of breed promotion by a number of British Morgan Horse Society members at shows and demonstrations). Today due to renewed interest and development in the breed's ability to participate in many other competitive spheres, breed shows offer a remarkable choice of divisions and classes. Working Stock Horse, Reining Horse, Cutting Horse (all Western performance classes), Hunter-Jumper, Roadster (under saddle or to a bike, a type of sulky), Dressage and Carriage Driving classes and more are provided and supported. The performance value of the Morgan is thus well recognized overall.

Saddleseat

Saddleseat is a style of riding similar to that once seen on Rotten Row, London, during the Regency period. This style was also adopted in the southern states of North America and today Saddlebreds, Tennessee Walkers, Arabs, Morgans and more recently Andalusians can be shown in this way in America.

Saddleseat follows the basics of all riding such as balance, levelness and lightness of the aids. The rider should be seated centrally in the saddle in a correct vertical position, knees touching the saddle at all times and the lower leg slightly away from the horse instead of curled around the girth. However, faults often seen are riders seated far back on the saddle with legs thrust out stiffly, far away from the horse's sides, in an attempt to show off and heighten the front action, often at the expense of hind action. This gives the horse an uphill, laboured appearance.

The saddle, ideally cut-back at the pommel, should have a flat seat and no panelling or knee rolls, similar to a show cob saddle, as this gives a more elegant view of the shoulder. In Britain many Morgan exhibitors use a cut-back dressage saddle of minimal padding. The show bridle is usually a long-shanked double bridle of the Weymouth type, with all leather pieces extremely fine and thin. Matching browbands and cavassons are used to display stable colours and designs and to highlight the appearance of the horse's head. Pelhams and snaffles are also allowed, although the snaffle is generally used on young horses beginning their show career.

Traditional dress is the Saddlesuit, which consists of ankle-flared Kentucky jodhpurs covering the boot, a long skirted jacket, a waistcoat (optional), a conventional shirt and tie and dark gloves. The jacket may match the jodhpurs or contrast in a lighter solid colour. Daytime headwear for ladies is a derby or bowler, while men often wear a soft trilby. Evening classes and championships allow top hats, bow ties and cummerbunds, and white gloves are correct for evening formals.

Morgan horses are traditionally shown Saddleseat in the following sections: Park, English Pleasure, Classic Pleasure and Road Hack. Whilst each section has specific requirements with regard to height of action, head and neck set, speed, displays of animation and collection and lightness, horses should still be obedient to the aids and well mannered. To ensure that the Morgan has a clear understanding of what is required a large proportion of his training is spent perfecting his performance on the ground through the use of long-reins and a training harness which encourages the horse to condition his muscles and adopt the desired self-carriage and motion.

The Park Morgan

The training of the Park Morgan is a very specialized and long-term process. It requires a horse of specific attitude, capability and talent. Hence it is not surprising to learn that the Park Morgan represents only one per cent of the Morgan population. When ridden, the Park Morgan should produce a picture of power, animation, lightness and unity with his rider. The Park Morgan class is often described as the 'show case' of the breed due to the horse's upheaded look, proud bearing and exuberant trot. The trot should exhibit a high but controlled step, which is fluid, light and airy yet

Multi Grand Champion Morgan show horse, the stallion Tarryall Gene Thiery ('Maestro') gives a balanced display of the Park Morgan in Britain, ridden by John Bulmer. (*Photo by Nicola Sutton, courtesy John and Angela Bulmer*)

powerful. The canter should be slow and collected, the walk a rapid, elastic pace, a two-time beat often being accepted by judges. When driven the Park horse is allowed more expression in the trot. Driven Park horses pull a light-weight show vehicle to seat one person, a Viceroy, similar to those which Hackneys are put to in the show ring. The lightness of this vehicle allows the horse to move freely, without hindrance.

Further information regarding the training, presentation and performance of the Park Morgan as well as comprehensive coverage of many other aspects of the breed can be found in *The Complete Morgan Horse* by Jane Mellin. Breed organizations will also help with enquiries.

The Pleasure Morgan

In the 1960s and 1970s, the description of a ridden Pleasure Morgan would be of a horse of longer outline and lower step than the Park Morgan, exhibiting impeccable manners, balance and tractability on a very light rein contact. Today the Pleasure Morgan must still display excellent manners (the most important factor), but should also have a degree of collection, be upheaded and expressive, and step as near to a level forearm in the trot as possible, with hocks moving and flexing well underneath. All paces must be displayed on a light contact and 'with attitude'. The walk should be an elastic four-beat pace, and the trot brisk and stylish, with the horse able to perform the Road Trot, a ground-covering pace of increased speed, in balance and on a light rein. The Pleasure driving horse must match up to all the requirements of a good road horse, possessing impeccable manners and abundant style, and must retain balance and stride in the Road Trot without any inclination to race.

Pleasure horses when driven pull a light-weight exercise cart called a Gerald, a type of vehicle that would be used for pleasure activities by the family.

For those who would like to become involved with the traditional showing styles of the performance Morgan, the Pleasure section would be the most advisable place to start as there are many classes which cater for the newcomer. The description 'Pleasure Morgan' must, in fact, be a reality in the show ring. This requirement encourages both breeders and trainers to produce quality representatives of the breed which also retain one of the Morgan's most fundamental characteristics, a tractable temperament.

7 Introduction of the Morgan to Great Britain

The first consignment of American Morgan horses, destined as foundation breeding stock and the primary ambassadors of a British Morgan breed society and register, arrived in Britain on 14 February 1975. For over 100 years importations of Morgan blood had occurred but not for these specific purposes, or with such publicity.

The initial spark for this event was struck by an American mare, Ballad of Goshen, purchased by Angela Conner Bulmer in 1957 while in America with her family as a girl. Angela, a well-known British artist and scupltress, returned to Britain in the 1960s to continue her artistic career, eventually to be reunited with Ballad whose importation, a surprise gift, inspired the foundation of the Morgan in Britain.

During her ageing years Ballad was settled at Monnington Court, Hereford, the home of Angela and her husband, John Bulmer. Wanting to continue the characteristics and qualities she felt were represented by Ballad and the Morgan breed, Angela began discussing the possibilities of importing a registered Morgan mare.

By 1970 discussion with family and friends developed into plans to combine the efforts of George Ivan Smith, Angela's stepfather, and Mrs Nancy Hedley-Dent of Northumberland, a friend made during Angela's years in America. This enthusiastic trio decided to purchase and import three foundation horses: two in-foal mares and a stallion.

Foundation horses

Four years of diligent searching and researching elapsed before the three foundation horses were found, with the aid of overwhelming generosity and support from many American contacts and friends. The unstinting help of Anne Boorman Canavan, Jeanne Mellin Herrick and Robert Brooks did not end with finding these first horses, but carried on into later importations and the development of the British Morgan Horse Society and its associated activities.

The two mares were Tarryall Cadenza, BMHS 1, AMHA 02877 (Applevale Cadence x She'll Do) and See Jay Melody, BMHS 2, AMHA 023049 (Broadwall Phyldon x Little Nugget), and the stallion was Pegasus Royal Pride, BMHS 3, AMHA 21909 (Topside Jolly Roger x Dainty Dot). Their pedigrees combined Lippitt, Government, Brunk and Western Working bloodlines of distinction, each individual possessing in abundance the traits and qualities characteristic of the

Tarryall Cadenza, an excellent example of a quality Morgan mare. (*Photo by J. Bulmer*)

Morgan breed. Time was not wasted in attaining publicity. Three days after the horses arrived at Monnington Court in 1975, 20 or so visitors attended a demonstration which was reported in the local and national press.

Tarryall Cadenza, a bay foaled on 12 April 1972, was bred by Dr Robert Edgar of Colorado. She was purchased by Angela Conner Bulmer as foundation mare for Monnington Morgans and was later given to Angela's husband John Bulmer. Sadly Cadenza conceived twin foals which did not survive their birth. She had won in-hand championships in the USA and accumulated many winnings at British Morgan shows in Pleasure saddle, English and Western, harness and in-hand classes, and she is retained by Monnington Morgans as a favourite and successful broodmare. Her first live foal was Monnington Jubilate (x Pegasus Royal Pride), foaled in 1977. Jubilate was the first British-bred Morgan foal, and she easily went on to prove the breeding prowess of both her sire and dam in her career as a sport horse and broodmare with owner Elizabeth Sharp. Cadenza's third daughter Monnington Descant (by Monnington Motif), foaled in 1982, is another example of her broodmare abilities. Descant, owned by Sealmaster Ltd, qualified for the Horse of the Year Show in 1993 for the Contours d'Elegance Harness Class.

See Jay Melody, a liver chestnut, foaled on 8 May 1972, was bred by C. and L. Jaques of Vermont. Melody was purchased by Nancy Hedley-Dent as foundation mare for the Bolbec Stud. She was retained at Monnington Court for 18 months to

Britain's first Park Morgan mare, See Jay Melody, seen here driven by Anne Huband to a viceroy at Shortflatt, Northumberland. (*Photo courtesy Nancy Hedley-Dent*)

produce her first foal, a filly, Bolbec Prima (1975–85), BMHS 4 (by Hanover Supercharger) and to aid a collective breed promotion programme before travelling with her foal to their Northumbrian home in 1976. Melody was Britain's first Park Saddle and Harness mare, attaining many successes at British Morgan shows with her trainer, Anne Huband, as well as in Concours d'Elegance and Private Driving classes in between broodmare duties. She has been the dam of show horses, sport horses and excellent breeding stock. She was first on lease and then gifted to the author in Lanarkshire, Scotland.

Pegasus Royal Pride (1971–85), a strapping 15.3 hand bay stallion, was foaled on 20 April 1971 and bred by J. and V. Muse of Colorado. Besides being a Morgan of great size, substance, type and character, Pegasus was the epitome of the versatile Morgan horse. He was originally purchased by George Ivan Smith as a gift for his daughter, Edda. However, after the arrival of another stallion in 1976 he was bought

Pegasus Royal Pride coming out of a water hazard at Osberton National Driving Trials, 1983. (*Photo by Equestrian Services Thorney*)

by Major Ronnie Hedley-Dent as the Bolbec foundation stallion, arriving in Northumberland in April 1977. Over the years Pegasus proved himself to be just the type of stallion the Hedley-Dents appreciated. He showed his skills at hunting, jumping, sidesaddle, dressage, endurance and all types of driving, and won many in-hand stallion championships at breed shows, where he also competed in Park and Pleasure Saddle classes. He was liberally shown in stallion parades in the north of England and in Scotland, also participating in many varied breed promotions.

In 1979 Pegasus competed with his talented trainer, Jane Davidson, on a BHS Golden Horseshoe Ride of 50 miles over the Hexham Moors, achieving a time of 7.92 m.p.h. to win the Silver Award, narrowly missing the Gold award by 0.08 m.p.h. His many successes were due in no small part to the teaching skills and humour exhibited during the bi-annual visits of the late Lee (Emily) Ferguson, USA, a top-level Morgan dressage rider, trainer and publicly recognized breed promoter.

However, Pegasus' true joy lay with the challenges of FEI Driving Trials and marathon events. In the hands of his new groom and trainer, Lesley Allen (née Sharp), his first FEI season in the summer of 1983 saw him attaining a high standard of performance, culminating in a fifth overall placing at the Osberton National Driving Championships. In 1985 he placed amongst the first six at the Windsor Driving Championships, and his death that same winter was a sad curtailment of a promising career.

As a sire Pegasus contributed many notable part-breds to the horse world: hunters, eventers, showjumpers, dressage and driving horses of size, substance, quality and athletic ability. His purebred stock, though renowned for their versatility, temperament and ability, were limited in number due to his northerly location, a handicap still affecting northern Morgan sires. Pegasus produced eight purebred offspring, six fillies and two colts. His first son, Bolbec Arpeggio, BMHS 7 (x See Jay Melody) carries on his line as a sire in Yorkshire, and his most notable daughter is of course Monnington Jubilate, described previously. Owned since a foal by Elizabeth Sharp of Lincolnshire, Jubilate has made her name among other things as a hunter, and in open competition as a sidesaddle mount and Western horse, the first Morgan to be chosen to represent Britain at the European Western Championships in Munich, West Germany in 1986. Sadly they were unable to attend due to lack of finances.

Another very successful daughter is Bolbec Bonnibel, BMHS 23, foaled in 1978 (x Rapidan Coquette), who was often mistaken for her sire when seen at driving events. Bonnibel proved her skill in ridden and driven events with her breeder, Nancy Hedley-Dent, and trainer Lesley Allen, being amongst the first six placed at the

Monnington Jubilate ('Spook') with her owner Liz Sharp up, at a Side Saddle Association demonstration, Belvoir Castle, May 1987. ((*Photo courtesy E. Sharp*)

Windsor Driving Championships in 1987, two years after her sire's success. Upon the Hedley-Dent's retirement shortly afterwards, Bonnibel was sold to Margareta Sundberg of Sweden and has become one of the top Single Harness Horses in three-part competition under FEI rules.

The collective achievements of Pegasus Royal Pride and his stock have been described in detail here as they undoubtedly position him as the most comprehensively and consistently campaigned British Morgan breeding stallion to date. His successes and his innate versatility are a tribute to his breeders, his owners and to those who were involved with his training and presentation, and not least to the Morgan breed itself.

In 1976 the importation of the striking black yearling colt, Tarryall Gene Thiery, heralded interesting developments in the British Morgan world. Tarryall Gene Thiery, BMHS 5, AMHA 29517 (Applevale Cadence x Michele's Desiree) was

86

foaled on 31 March 1975. Bred by Dr Robert Edgar of Colorado, his pedigree shows him to be of 50 per cent Lippitt breeding. He is an official half brother to the mare Tarryall Cadenza, though they share further family ties in the Lippitt-bred portion of their pedigrees through their dams' lines.

To guarantee his purchase, a syndicate consisting of Elizabeth Sharp, Major Hedley-Dent, Elspeth Gill and John Bulmer was formed. This was later dissolved and the stallion was put in the joint ownership of Angela Conner Bulmer and Ms E. Smith, while Major Hedley-Dent instead acquired Pegasus Royal Pride. Thus the black stallion, which rapidly gained recognition under the name 'Maestro', headed Monnington Morgan's foundation breeding programme. He became the most influential British Morgan sire to date, having sired at least 37 per cent of all homebred, purebred foals by 1988.

The British Morgan Horse Society

The British Morgan Horse Society was formed in 1975. Within two years the Society had opened a Stud Book, with plans for blood typing all purebred Morgan horses, and had organized the Youth Group and breed shows, newsletters and eventually a magazine. This was quite an accomplishment, assisted financially and with considerable organizational effort by founder members, and an increasing body of supporters and friends. In 1978 affiliation with the British Horse Society was formally achieved.

The social aspect of the Society has been a top priority for many members who participate in specially organized events with or without horses. The membership in 1992 was approximately 200, 100 of whom are Morgan owners. Membership growth has been slow, due, perhaps, to the limited availability of Morgans. Especially in the early years, few mature Morgan horses were for sale on the open market, sales generally being of foals and youngsters.

Today, due to the growing success and involvement of the breed in open competition, sales of all age groups of Morgan horses are increasingly being directed towards the open market and a broader ownership.

Registrations

The Stud Book was opened in 1975, as the British Ministry of Agriculture refused breed recognition unless the Morgan had its own British-based register. In January 1988 an application was made to the AMHA for reciprocity of registration, as until then Morgans had to be registered in both countries to retain their breed credibility. A reciprocal agreement was achieved in February 1989.

> Other countries with Morgans must register through the AMHA, BMHS or the Canadian Livestock Registry. The Registrations of Morgans must be done according to the rules and regulations of the AMHA to preserve and protect the integrity of the breed. Canada and Britain have adopted our rules and were able to enter into a reciprocal agreement on this basis. Essentially we do not encourage many small registries to start without a strong basis of support as was the case with both Britain and Canada. (*AMHA correspondence*)

Between 1975 and 1987 approximate population figures of purebred Morgans, as shown in the *Directory of Morgan Horses in Great Britain* (1988), had increased from 3 to 210, an average increase of 17 per year. In that time the number of owners increased from approximately 6 to 90, an increase which occurred mainly in the 1980s. These figures may at first suggest that progress was rather slow. However, only a minor portion of a growing ownership were in a position to breed and import Morgan horses. Up until 1988, out of a total 136 mares and fillies, 61 were imported. Of these imported mares, 45 bred foals (approximately 18 of them were imported in foal) and eight of their British-bred female offspring also bred foals. Within a 12-year period a total of 134 Morgans were foaled and registered in Britain, nature maintaining a relatively even distribution of 75 fillies and 59 colts. Additional importations included one gelding and 13 stallions. These stallions and seven of their male offspring sired 116 foals, accounting for 65 of the fillies and 51 of the colts mentioned above.

From January 1988 to January 1992 registrations increased by a total of 104, reaching the grand total of 314 registrations. Therefore during those four years the annual average doubled to 34 Morgans being either born or imported to an owner and breedership of approximately 100 people! By 1993 totals exceeded 350 registrations.

One of the most far-seeing decisions Angela Conner Bulmer made as BMHS President was to institute blood typing for all purebred Morgan horses prior to their acceptance for registration. She organized this before any other British breed society or the AMHA adopted it, early recognizing the need to safeguard the breed in the future. It was mandatory by 1981.

A Part-Bred Register and an Anglo-Morgan Register are also maintained by the BMHS. Mrs Gillian Eyre handled all registrations for many years as BMHS

Registrar. She was especially concerned that all Part-Bred and Anglo-Morgans in Britain should be registered as youngsters, so as to validate future sales information and their eligibility for the rapid development of breed and performance classes held throughout the country for foreign and part-bred American breeds. The Anglo-Morgan Register accepts horses of 50 per cent registered Thoroughbred and 50 per cent registered Morgan breeding. The Part-Bred Register accepts horses containing registered Morgan breeding to a minimum of 25 per cent Morgan blood.

Breed shows and classes

The first County-level horse show to hold Morgan classes affiliated to the BMHS was the Hertfordshire County Show in 1979. The day was miserable, with tractors sinking deep in mud as they towed horseboxes, cars and trailers in and out of the gate. The showground looked like a war zone. I have often wondered what the public and other show competitors thought of the enthusiastic, mud-caked, dripping but smiling Morgan owners and helpers (their teeth probably the only completely shining part of them), attired in dress alien to the British contingent, their horses tacked up in traditional American show harness and saddlery, who did their best to cope with the adverse conditions.

A brave start indeed! Mud-spattered bowler hats, long saddlesuit jackets, rolled up Kentucky jodhpurs and saturated jodhpur boots suffered! Every possible Morgan owner had been appealed to to make the effort to attend with their horses, supporting the BMHS and the breed. Perhaps the most humorous aspect of the preparations before the show was the nail-biting wait for some of the tack (especially ordered for the event from American saddlers) to arrive in time for the big day, especially when it was found that the delay was due to it having to be exported from saddlers in Britain first before being sent back to Britain! However, these problems do not exist today as various British saddlers are able to supply specific American styles of tack and harness.

Hertfordshire County Show still holds Morgan classes, as does the Three Counties Show and the Spillers Show at Ardingly. The American All Breeds Show, usually held at Stoneleigh and organized by Gillian Eyre since 1986, offers participation to all breeds of horse under American rules of judging and includes a comprehensive list of classes ranging from Hunter, Dressage, Western and Saddleseat as well as in-hand classes for American breeds and part-breds. This show is well supported by Quarter Horses, Morgans, the colour breeds and more recently the Saddlebreds, with added support coming from many other breeds and types which participate in the performance classes.

In the early days farm shows, scattered throughout the country (the most northerly ones held in Northumberland by John and Joanna Caulfield of Newlands Grange Morgans), catered for the showing interests of the BMHS membership. They incorporated a comprehensive assortment of classes to suit novice horses, the novice rider/driver and junior competitors, with the accent on having an enjoyable time. However, since the nucleus of Morgans lived in the south of England at that time the northern shows dwindled, unable through lack of support to finance the required invitations to American judges if they wished their classes to be affiliated to the Society. Although there are now two British-based Morgan judges who generously provide their expertise and skills, American judges are still predominantly requested by the Society to judge at Morgan shows.

In 1992 and 1993 an end-of-year Championship Show was organized and held near Chester. It has proved very popular with its list of classes which cater for many types of breed performance. It is hoped that this show will become an annual event situated in a central area of the country.

Classes presently provided at the majority of breed shows are Park, Pleasure Saddle and Harness (as briefly described in Chapter 6) and in-hand, with a growing accent on equitation in the ridden classes. However, classes at County shows, though they provide increased public promotion, are often restricted by time limits and a lack of ring space to ensure safety for the increasing numbers who participate in harness classes.

BMHS promotions

In 1978 a team was formed by the BMHS to promote the Morgan through a traditional display at shows and other venues. Other promotions via radio, newspaper, magazines and television have greatly aided the Morgan cause in Britain. One such televised promotion was a film made by John Bulmer, a professional cameraman, entitled *The Artist's Horse*. It was shown on the South Bank Show on 1 April 1978, introduced by Melvin Bragg to an estimated five and a half million viewers.

In 1985 the BMHS Team was invited to perform at the Horse of the Year Show, Wembley. A team of 20 horses and almost 50 people contributed their efforts to produce a stylish and romantic display of Morgans ridden in traditional Morgan style and driven to elegant carriages, accompanied by appropriate music provided by

BMHS Team display at Castle Howard, 1989. (*Photo courtesy Anna and Richard Fisher*)

Major Kenny and his band. The display received complimentary reviews, such as 'enormously popular' (*Hare and Hound*) and 'Charming and romantic . . . a joy to the eye and ear' (*Country Life*). The team trials are open to anyone in the BMHS. The purpose of the Team so far has been to produce a musical ridden and driven display of romance, style and elegance. Approximately one-third of the BMHS membership have been involved with the Display Team at one time or another.

The Youth Group

Youngsters in the BMHS are well catered for. Members of the BMHS aged 21 and under are provided with a club and living quarters at Monnington Court, various national activities, training schemes and a scholarship linked to an exchange scheme

BMHS Youth Group Clinic held at Monnington Court, Hereford. Mary Woolverton (from the USA) is seen here helping the children. (*Photo courtesy BMHS*)

with the AMHA, the winning candidates able to venture into each other's country of Morgandom. The success of the first years of the Youth Group are attributable to the dedication, generosity and enthusiasm of Mrs Nina Bacon, now resident in the USA.

8 Profile of Morgan horses in Great Britain

As an increasing number of people have become associated with the Morgan in Great Britain, importation levels have remained healthy, new breeding programmes have been established, individual breedings have increased and existing breeding programmes have continued to develop. With this growth the breed can be better evaluated.

The general consensus, gained from visiting American judges, owners and breeders, and from the British Morgan community itself, is that breed standards are high overall and well maintained by importers and breeders alike. As the breed becomes involved in a wider range of performance, here too better evaluation can be made of progress in many and varied disciplines. Importing horses is costly, and developing a characteristic and adept breed population, when breeding is almost entirely subject to personal preference, takes time, study and a measure of fortuity. Therefore the most sensible and economical strategy is to import representatives of the breed which meet both performance and conformation ideals as closely as possible. In the main this strategy has been employed. Whether fortuitous or studied, it has enabled British breeders to become increasingly selective and purposeful.

Choosing a small but comprehensive selection of Morgan horses in Great Britain for discussion posed several problems for me. I questioned myself as to why, within a relatively small population, there seemed to be so many horses to consider. The answer was simple. Due to the breed's versatility, it appeals to many varied needs and interests. I found many horses to be of significance, whether as receivers of public, competitive or breeding recognition, as the personal friend of an individual or family, or as a combination of all these.

So I have tried to provide an overall picture of the breed as it is found in Britain. I have included a selection of both imported and British-bred stock and examples of their progeny throughout the country. Examples of other British Morgans are to be found in the previous chapter and following ones.

Certainly the small population of Morgan horses in Britain makes it a minority breed, but the achievements and influence of individuals are not so minor, even though they are often guided initially by novice hands.

The majority of Morgans populate the central and southern regions of England, but increasing numbers are to be found in northern England, with small numbers in Wales and over the Scottish border in Dumfries-shire, Lanarkshire, Stirlingshire,

Tayside and further north in Ross-shire. Both northern and southern Ireland have recently increased their interest, and the islands of Guernsey and Jersey support a handful of Morgan horses between them.

Kent

The potential of the Morgan was realized soon after its British introduction. Waseeka Firecracker, BMHS 13 (Waseeka's Here Tiz x Windcrest Sentimental Lady), one of Britain's most senior stallions, was the first Morgan to compete successfully in British open competition. 'Cracker', a liver chestnut stallion bred by Waseeka Farm of Ashland, Massachusetts, USA, was foaled in 1967. He is owned by H. B. Phillips but is in the care of Nan and Tony Phillips of Ionian Morgans, Kent.

Cracker's story is an unusual one. He arrived in Britain in 1977 in exchange for a Clifton Gig and show harness sent to the USA. His first British owner was Mrs Sherman, an experienced show driver, and soon after his arrival Cracker took part in the Queen's Silver Jubilee Drive. Also in 1977 he won the Horse and Hound Cup for the Novice Championship and the Spillers Trophy at the British Driving Society Show, Smith's Lawn, Windsor. Cracker was later sold on and did not re-emerge into the show ring until his purchase by the Phillips family in 1983.

Cracker was then shown at BMHS shows – in-hand and in Park Saddle classes – and participated in Society clinics, demonstrations and displays. He had the honour of being the lead horse in the BMHS Team displays performed at the Wembley Horse of the Year Show in 1985. In 1987, after four years in the public eye and at the age of 20, Cracker retired from the ring as Grand Champion Park Horse at the Herts County show.

Waseeka Firecracker's contribution as a sire of purebred Morgans was limited during his years of obscurity, but he has sired many fine offspring of athletic ability and substance. His ability to pass on his style of movement rendered him a popular choice for those interested in the Park horse classes. His most successful Park horse daughter is Bolbec Diva (x See Jay Melody) bred by Nancy Hedley-Dent of Northumberland and owned by Dawn Sharif of Dorneywood Morgans in Buckinghamshire. Diva has also been very successful at show jumping and cross-country in open competition, also enjoying the hunting field and sidesaddle.

Waseeka Firecracker's ancestry contains many of the horses and lines mentioned in Chapter 4. In the third generation of his pedigree there appear Waseeka's Nocturne and Upwey Ben Don; in the fourth generation, Starfire, Upwey Benn Quietude,

Parade, Upwey King Benn (with two further crosses in the fifth generation), Quietude (with two further crosses in the fifth generation) and Cornwallis, who also appears in the fifth generation as the sire of Parade.

Hereford

The black stallion, Tarryall Gene Thiery, BMHS 5 (Applevale Cadence x Michele's Desiree) is to date Britain's most influential sire. He was foaled in 1975, bred by Tarryall Farm of Littleton, Colorado, USA, and imported in 1976, later becoming the foundation stallion for Monnington Morgans, Hereford, the home of one of his joint owners, Angela Conner Bulmer, and her husband. Between 1979 and 1987 this horse, known and promoted as 'Maestro' in Britain, sired 24 foals for the farm and a further 19 to visiting mares, which together accounted for well over one-third of British foals born between those dates. Obviously this concentration of a single sire's blood could have unbalanced the national genetic pool, but conscientious breeding decisions and new importations prevented this situation from occurring.

'Maestro' achieved his success at BMHS shows. He holds a long list of BMHS Championships for in-hand, Park Saddle and Harness classes. In 1980, the only time shown in the Concours d'Elegance at Smith's Lawn, Windsor, 'Maestro' was one of six equal winners qualifying for the World Championships.

A successful 'Maestro' son, Monnington Conductor (x Springervale Kristen), excelling in Private Drive and Concours d'Elegance. (*Photo by Equestrian Services Thorney*)

The efforts of Angela and John and Monnington Morgans deserve special mention here. They were the largest single importer of Morgan mares and the largest consistent Morgan breeding operation for many years. They invested great efforts and funds to establish a breed base and opportunities for other Morgan owners, and to help fulfil the stated aims of the BMHS: to develop specialized breed shows to maintain a separate identity for the breed. To promote these efforts many of the farm's quality horses were sold, and the farm's own breeding goals may have been restricted in the process. However, an advantage which emerged from the selling of many of Maestro's offspring was that they have succeeded in a wider range of pursuits than their sire competed in, and have thus extended both his reputation and that of the breed.

The 50 per cent Lippitt breeding of Tarryall Gene Thiery is contributed by his dam, a purebred Lippitt Morgan recorded in the Lippitt Register under number 606. His sire traces back to the Lippitt stallion Cornwallis through Sealect of Windcrest by Pecos, and also to Jubilee King (the Brunk-bred sire) through Sealect of Windcrest's dam, Janee.

'Maestro' has been a major influence in breed promotions, performing alongside other Morgans owned and bred by Monnington in the BMHS Team displays, many of whom are his easily recognizable black offspring. He was ridden by John Bulmer during the Morgan displays performed by the Team at the Horse of the Year Show in 1985, and he has participated in the numerous clinics and demonstrations held at Monnington Court, always pulling in the crowds with his gentle appeal.

Worcester

Two close friends sharing a common breeding goal, Janet Ditcham and Gillian Eyre, each run Morgan breeding farms on adjoining land surrounded by lovely hill riding country near Kidderminster, Worcester.

Bluestone Farm, the larger of the two enterprises, is owned by Janet Ditcham and the home of her black foundation stallion, Whippoorwill Osiris, BMHS 40 (Bald Mt Black Cloud x Whippoorwill Isis). He was foaled in 1978 and bred by McCollough Farm (Whippoorwill Morgans) of Old Lyme, Connecticut, USA. Osiris was imported to Britain in 1979 with the purpose of carrying on the Whippoorwill motto, 'Family Morgans with an enviable show record'. Osiris has fulfilled this motto well, with winnings in hand, under saddle in Saddleseat, Western and English classes, endurance, dressage and varied jumping events. He has also participated in BMHS

Whippoorwill Osiris, Britain's second most influential breeding stallion to date, with his owner Janet Ditcham.

clinics and displays and in area riding club activities. He is highly regarded as a true ambassador of Morgan versatility.

Between 1982 and 1991 Osiris sired over 50 foals, 27 of them purebred Morgans. This figure had significantly increased by 1994, making him the second most influential sire. He stands at 14.2 hands and is also widely in demand as a part-bred sire, distributing his charms amongst a large range of mares from Welsh ponies to a 16.2 hand Irish Draught mare! The winnings of his offspring in BMHS and open competition in England and Scotland are ample evidence of his success and influence as a breeding stallion.

The Bluestone breeding programme began in 1988. The farm's breeding policy is to breed for those stirling Morgan virtues such as durability, soundness, kindness, common-sense and good looks. Specially selected broodmares were found. A relatively recent addition to the broodmare band, helping to ensure these breeding goals, is Dunoir Montana, BMHS 127 (Robbins Night Flight x H-Bar Panama), foaled in

Dunoir Montana, a splendid example of refinement without loss of breed type, substance and balance in the Morgan mare; and (*below*) Ted Ledger with H-Bar Panama and her first British-born foal, Dunoir Laddie, the first palomino Morgan to be born in Britain.

1983 and bred by E. J. Ledger of Sittingbourne, Kent. This mare is both striking and substantial, dun in colour and totally descended from Brunk (Mid-west) and Western Working blood lines. She would stir envy in the hearts of any serious breeder interested in maintaining breed substance and beauty. Her dam, H-Bar Panama, a palomino, was one of two mares Mr Ledger imported in 1982, ten years after receiving them as a wedding present whilst he was working in north-west Wyoming, USA. Panama and her buckskin (dun) herd companion, Tigres, were bred by George A. Cross and Son of Dubois, Wyoming, and born on the range which rose over 8500 feet above sea level. Their arrival in Britain sparked off a lot of interest due to their colouring and breeding. Both mares have the stallion Chingadero in their pedigrees (Tigres is sired by him), a rare grey Morgan who also sired black foals to form the 'Black Horse Troop', a Masonic group dedicated to raising money for charity by parading in various US cities.

Marches Morgan Farm, a significantly smaller enterprise than Bluestone, is owned by Gillian Eyre. It is unique because it is the home of the only purebred Lippitt Morgan presently in Britain. Rohan Camellia, BMHS 49 and number 1056 in the Lippitt Register (Royalton Ashline x Moro Hill's Emelyn), was bred by Clara Hendin of Rohan Morgans and foaled in 1978 when the farm was based in Randolph Centre, Vermont, USA. The mare was imported to Britain by Gillian in 1980 and has so far produced at least four foals to four different British Morgan stallions. The main aims of Marches Morgans is to maintain the influence of Lippitt blood in future generations and to breed purebred Lippitt foals in the future, initially from Camellia, by

Gillian Eyre and her purebred Lippitt mare Rohan Camellia, pictured here as a two year old.

importing frozen semen from the USA. However, the farm has been instrumental in maintaining original breed characteristics, temperament and versatility by breeding from excellent foundation broodmare stock.

Two outstanding broodmares to produce foals for the farm, and for their previous owners, were the early foundation mares (both now deceased) Just-A-Nod Exodus, BMHS 8 (U.C. Troubadour x Emeralds Top Lady) and Novanna Ethan L, BMHS 20 (Merry Ethan x Keomah Laurie L). Both broodmares, foaled in 1965 and 1964 respectively, were imported in foal by Monnington Morgans in 1978 with accompanying progeny. They were excellent producers of breeding stock, show winners and versatile sport and pleasure Morgans. Their individual breeding combined a successful mixture of Lippitt, Government and Western Working lines.

Just-A-Nod Exodus, a mare of good 'old' breeding and strong and substantial in appearance, produced at least seven foals in Britain for four separate breeders. She arrived in Britain with her colt foal Monnington Mozart at foot and in foal to U.C. Marquis, by whom she produced a colt, Monnington Motif, who went on to sire two fillies and two colts before being gelded after 1983. Motif's first foal, a filly, Monnington Descant, qualified for the Horse of the Year Show (Concours d'Elegance) in 1993 along with a number of other horses owned by Tessa Malcolm Brown and Sealmaster Ltd. Exodus was then purchased by Gillian Mercer who bred Calcutt Elms Tornado (by Tarryall Gene Thiery), a gelding owned by Mary Kirby and campaigned very successfully by her in long distance and endurance rides. The last colt produced by Exodus, the second of her foals for Marches Morgans, was Marches Just Ethan (by Tarryall Gene Thiery). He was foaled in 1986 and was sold to Susan Clyde of Craigs Stud, Co. Antrim, Northern Ireland, Ireland's first-known registered Morgan and foundation stallion.

Novanna Ethan L, a great producer of fillies, had her last foal, Marches Gem Athena (by Whippoorwill Osiris) in 1988 at the age of 24. Four of Novanna's daughters have been the foundation mares for various studs throughout the country: Littletown Flirt, BMHS 19 (by Ledgemere Alert), imported with her dam, for Belmont Morgans in North Yorkshire; Monnington Bolero, BMHS 53 (by Tarryall Gene Thiery), for Lionhart Morgans of East Essex; Monnington Calypso, BMHS 76 (by Tarryall Gene Thiery) for Landside Morgans near Manchester; and Gemini Sapphire, BMHS 126 (by Tarryall Gene Thiery) for Asoka Farm also near Manchester. Novanna's first British-born foal, though bred in the USA, was the colt Monnington Andante, BMHS 38 (by Ledgemere Alert), who is Scotland's only Morgan breeding stallion and the foundation stallion of Mountain Top Morgans in

Calcutt Elms Tornado ('Mr Stubbs'), runner-up for the Endurance Horse and Pony Society Wessex Group Trophy in May 1988, ridden by his owner Mary Kirby. (*Photo courtesy Mary Kirby*)

Lanarkshire. Thus Novanna Ethan L has made an important contribution to the development of British breeding and performance stock.

Shropshire

A Morgan farm based in Shropshire is Lagden Farm in Bishops Castle, the home of Rosita Hamar, a well-established breeder of Thoroughbred performance horses. Rosita's involvement with Morgans began through her friendship with Miss Yvonne Gregory (probably Britain's most senior Morgan owner and breeder at a youthful 80 years plus), who between 1988 and 1990 purchased Belmont Fantasy, a British-bred mare, and H.C. Mays Reflection, a very typey mare imported to Scotland by Anne Taylor. These mares produced both pure and part-bred stock at Lagden, so that evaluation of their offspring could be made. A fortuitous meeting and ensuing friendship with two highly respected breeders of Morgan performance horses, Charles and Charlotte Ross of Taproot Farm, Hinesburg, Vermont, provided Rosita with the opportunity to search for a stallion.

To suit the high performance standards of the British competition market and to aid promotion of the breed in this sphere, it was felt that a stallion of superior size and athletic ability, combined with type and quality, needed to be found. In 1990 Rosita visited the Rosses with this purpose in mind, and organized the purchase not only of one young stallion, Taproot Green Mt Boy, but also a weanling colt, Taproot Yankee Doodle. Both horses arrived in Britain in 1991.

Taproot Green Mt Boy (Deer Run Command x Taproot Copper Iris), stable name Ethan, was bought for Yvonne Gregory. Ethan was foaled in 1987 and stands 15.2 hands. He is fortunate that the worth of his breeding (based on 'old' Government

Taproot Green Mt Boy in basic training. (*Photo courtesy Yvonne Gregory*)

lines) has been proven through the achievements of his full brother Taproot Command Pilot, who was chosen for training by the US Olympic Horse Trials Coach, Denny Emerson. Ethan's full blood brother, Taproot Flagship, is an outstanding dressage competitor rapidly working his way to advanced levels in the United States with Jackie Ross Qua. By 1993, as a six year old, it became evident that Ethan had inherited the same performance potential. During his first serious competitive season he proved his ability and boldness at cross-country events, apparently unworried by a variety of tricky situations. Rosita, his trainer, was very much encouraged and feels hopeful that as his skill develops he will be fast enough to achieve the times which advanced competition requires. His jumping ability was also recognized in show jumping and working hunter events, where he easily obtained top placings. Interestingly, in hunter classes against typically British competition, Ethan has impressed the judges enough to stay in the ribbons. His manners and obedience have also made him successful in riding horse classes, and it is evident that he has potential for more advanced dressage work as well. Taproot Green Mt Boy has sired two purebred foals for Miss Gregory and a small number of part-breds for Rosita.

Taproot Yankee Doodle (Taproot Command Pilot x Taproot Twin Flower) was foaled in 1990 and is owned by Rosita. His well-grown appearance as a weanling cemented her decision to buy him as a future performance horse and sire. In 1993, at three years old, he measured a full 15.3 hands with expectations of at least 16 hands. He is being given time to grow and fill out his large frame before he follows a similar training programme as Taproot Green Mt Boy.

As a yearling Yankee Doodle was shown in Open Hunter Youngstock and Working Hunter Youngstock, winning championships and reserve championships. His first purebred foal was expected in 1994.

At the time of writing it is too early to assess what contribution these stallions will make to the breed. They are unique, however, in that they are the first Morgan stallions to be imported which have been explicitly evaluated for their performance and for the development of pure and part-bred stock, and they are certainly of interest to the breed's future in Britain, especially now that the Morgan is being increasingly recognized for its competitive potential against other breeds.

Lagden Farm are successfully crossing these stallions with their large Thoroughbred mares in the hope of producing Anglo-Morgans with competition and sport potential, capable of maintaining their place amongst the popular warmbloods of various types. They have found that the best type of foal from this cross is being produced by fairly substantial blood mares, the foals inheriting the sharp intelligence and bright, active attitude of their sire, and also, very importantly, the tractable temperament.

Lancashire

Robbins Night Flight ('Topper'), BMHS 99 (Top Flight x Dorthea Allen) is another of Britain's senior stallions, owned for many years by Peggy Litton of Barbrook Farm, Worsely, Manchester. Night Flight is unique in that he is the only Morgan sire in Britain bred wholly from Mid-western (Brunk) and Western Working lines. He was foaled in 1967 in Missouri, USA, bred by L. D. and O. R. Robbins. His last American owner, Matilda Chappell, also of Missouri, saw him through a successful show career, including a Grand National Championship, before selling him to Keith Quick, one of Britain's early owners and importers. It was felt that with his breeding, above average size, tractability and athleticism, he would make a significant contribution to the development of the Morgan in Britain, and this he has done by siring a

Robbins Night Flight, a senior British Morgan sire descended wholly from Brunk and Western Working lines.

Five-day old colt foal (born June 1993) by Robbins Night Flight out of Gemini Sapphire.

good number of quality pure and part-bred foals, easily recognizable as 'Topper' offspring.

His sire, Top Flight, was by the famous Flyhawk, who was bred by Joseph C. Brunk. Photographs indicate a close likeness between father and son. The appearance of Robbins Night Flight has also been likened to that of Flyhawk, but though the resemblance is certainly there he is of slightly bigger frame, and old photographs suggest that he has inherited characteristics very comparable to Go Hawk, Flyhawk's sire. Flyhawk himself was a remarkable individual and a great influence on the breed. He was a top ranch and pleasure horse, and later a show horse. The dam of Top Flight was Sentola, a full sister of Jubilee King, another highly acclaimed sire bred by the Brunk family. Certainly the look of the Flyhawk line is noticeable in the offspring of Robbins Night Flight. His half sister, Robbins Top Duchess, was also imported and was owned by Pauline Lumb of Yorkshire until the mare's death. She also strongly resembled Flyhawk breeding.

'Topper' is unusual because of his multi-breed home, where the breeding prefix of 'Asoka' is used for Morgans, Iberians, Arabians and Lippizaners. The farm run by Peggy Litton and the prefix 'Asoka' have been associated with breeding livestock, but latterly they have concerned themselves with display work, concentrating on the Classical Breeds and the performance of Classical High School, with a few of the most talented horses performing Circus High School. Pennington Othello, BMHS 159 (Robbins Night Flight x Monnington Aria), participates in the Asoka training and display programme, performing Classical High School movements. Othello and Night Flight, who was then aged 23, went up to Scotland in 1990 to join other Morgan horses to promote the breed in a Gala of Western Horsemanship held in Glasgow. Othello's contribution was to perform work in-hand on long reins and Night Flight was ridden Western and as a Parade horse.

Night Flight's first American-bred filly made Grand Champion Mare in Illinois in 1973, and his British-bred offspring are doing extremely well in FEI driving events, cross-country, dressage and show jumping, as well as being enjoyed as family horses. The majority of his foals have inherited their sire's size and large frame and it is accepted that they need a little extra time to reach maturity, but when they do the results are impressive. Night Flight has also contributed excellent bone, substance, balance and athleticism to his progeny and a generous workmanlike attitude which renders them all-round prospects. His 1993 foal, a black colt bred by Peggy Litton, is out of the Asoka Farm's mare Gemini Sapphire (Tarryall Gene Thiery x Novanna Ethan L), and looks to be the one to carry on from his sire.

A close neighbour of the Asoka Stud is Landside Morgans, owned and run by Walter and Anne James of Leigh, Manchester. This farm is one of a handful in Britain that have managed to establish a serious breeding programme of reasonable size and continuity. Anne and Walter, a veterinary surgeon, have been involved with Morgans for over a decade, and are dedicated breeders with clear intentions: to produce Morgans of the original Justin Morgan type, temperament and versatility to suit the British market and to maintain these intentions over succeeding generations.

Robbins Night Flight was the catalyst for it all. Walter visited Peggy Litton's stud in his veterinary capacity and was immediately struck by Topper's imposing appearance and manners, so much so that he returned with his wife, Anne, who was equally impressed. In 1982 they purchased their first Morgan, a mare, Monnington Calypso, BMHS 76 (Tarryall Gene Thiery x Novanna Ethan L). Due to Walter's 34 years of veterinary experience and Anne's lifelong association with horses, they put together a selection of broodmares that certainly no one else could have consciously chosen! Of these mares Monnington Calypso had contracted opthalmia (a disease which affects the eye), though this did not hinder her from being a Junior In-hand Champion, being trained for both English and Western, and also being used as a

BMHS Youth horse. She proved to be an outstanding broodmare and enjoys life virtually free from attacks of the disease which left her blind in one eye. Bald Mt Pansy, BMHS 85 (Andon Vigil Charlie x Penny Royal Trilight), imported as a foal by Monnington Morgans in 1980, and a more recent addition to the Landside broodmare band, is also blind in one eye. Country Dusty Lady, BMHS 63 (Country March Squire x Devan Dusty), another of the mares imported by Keith Quick in 1980 and also the dam of Glenns Phoenix, a 1982 sport horse gelding owned by Susan Brotherstone of Edinburgh, Scotland, was barren for the next nine years but surprised everybody eventually! Kinsman Cotton Queen, BMHS 41 (Applevale Kinsman x Dal Mor Cotton Candy), also an imported mare and owned since her arrival until 1991 by Sue Buck of Scotland, would in all probability have died in labour in spring 1993 had not Walter's veterinary skill detected a very unusual problem.

In 1984 the Jameses imported Tarheel Sweet Accord, BMHS 160 (Casey Tibbs x Robbins Top Duchess, who was separately imported in the same year), in foal to Olympus Mr Promise (by UVM Promise). She produced Landside Mr Promise, BMHS 164, in 1985, a combination of the Western Working lines they admired in Robbins Night Flight and the Government lines through UVM Promise. He was the foundation stallion they had hoped for. To the Jameses, Promise epitomizes what they feel to be Morgan type, with the breeding, conformation and presence to complement their mares.

The farm maintains approximately 17 Morgans at any one time, a large portion of

No brandy for me? Landside Masterpiece (Landside Mr Promise x Bald Mt Pansy) and friend.

Tarheel Sweet Accord with Landside Mr Promise at foot.

these youngstock. Individual planning is given to each foal, and any sales are based upon future owners wanting an all-purpose family and using horse that just happens to look good too. The horses at Landside have been very successful in open competition as well as in the breed show ring, proving their versatility, but Anne and Walter maintain the view that 'pretty show horses are of neither use nor ornament' unless they can fit into the world at large. Strict evaluation is made of each colt's stallion status and this will not be maintained unless they believe him to carry the highest percentage of desirable breed traits. Landside Music Man, BMHS 214, foaled in 1987 and owned by Clare Unsworth, is a good example of a quality and versatile Landside gelding. He has been successful in breed and open competition, and as a six year old

108

in 1993 qualified for a BHS Event. He is by the late Townsend First Edition (Robbins Night Flight x Arduns Neva) and out of Monnington Calypso, making him a second-generation British-bred Morgan.

These strict and purposeful views have attracted interest from potential owners and breeders of other countries. The Jameses have been instrumental in the establishment of breeding enterprises in Germany and Ireland, with their interest in aiding international breed development going beyond basic sales. Arduns Neva, BMHS 30 (Anneigh Dark Cloud x Neva of Dickie), foaled in 1974 and another of Keith Quick's magical imports during the early years of the breed's development, is a truly inter-

A truly
international
mare, Arduns
Neva,
with Anne James
of Landside
Morgans. (*Photo
by Anthony
Reynolds*)

national horse, a foundation broodmare for Britain and now for Germany. She is an ideal Morgan mare, a winner of Breed Championships in the USA and Britain, and a versatile family horse in three countries. Believing that breeding programmes must be established by quality foundation stock, the Jameses not only decided to sell Neva to Andreas Zang, but personally delivered her to Aschaffenburg, Germany, in foal to Landside Mr Promise, and accompanied by a Landside filly, which was later sold on to another German owner. Neva did the honours and delivered a much wanted colt foal, Schnuddel Mr Promise. To maintain Neva's breeding contribution the Jameses have retained one of her daughters. To Ireland they sold Landside Flirt (U.C. Echo x Littletown Flirt), a granddaughter of the great broodmare Novanna Ethan L, and a colt is planned to follow in the future.

Northern England

The north of England, a region well known for its horse and pony breeding industry, is also noted for its active support of all forms of equine competition, pleasure pursuits and sport. The region's landscape is varied and offers ideal opportunities for the development of any native or newly introduced breed. The expanse of hill and dale is especially suitable for the Morgan horse, whose stamina and endurance evolved initially in a similar environment in North America, though both winter and summer weather are more extreme there.

In 1976 the Bolbec Stud of Northumberland, covered in greater detail in the previous chapter, brought the first Morgans to the north and bred and competed with them over a ten-year period. This stud, which also breeds Thoroughbreds, hunters and eventers, was particularly influential in promoting both the versatility and the overall sport potential of the Morgan, especially in FEI driving, with two generations of their horses: their foundation stallion Pegasus Royal Pride and his daughter Bolbec Bonnibel.

Between 1980 and 1992 ten Morgans – three stallions and seven mares – were imported to the north from America, helping to increase the population of the area to at least 24 Morgans by 1992. They are distributed amongst approximately ten owners. Perhaps distance from the majority of breed shows and the ample equine opportunities provided in the north has been one of the reasons why owners place more emphasis on regional pleasure and competitive activities than on preparing for the breed show ring. Competitive interests range from Private Driving and FEI Combined Driving to endurance riding, jumping, dressage and so on. Today the majority of Morgan owners are located in Northumberland and Co. Durham. As youngstock matures and the skills and interests of owners broaden, Morgans are regularly seen at competitive events, and it is usual to see one or two Morgan stallions representing the breed at the increasingly popular Stallion Viewing Parades.

In 1982 Kenneth Whitehead of Penrith, Cumbria, imported a yearling colt, Hartland Defiance, and a filly, Saddleback Samantha, with plans to breed from the pair, as both horses were from very successful show and breeding stock. Unfortunately Saddleback Samantha, BMHS 82 (Saddleback Supreme x Glamorgan Clivia) took a long time to comply with these plans, but produced a filly, Sockbridge Legacy, in 1992 and a colt in 1993, both by Defiance.

Hartland Defiance, BMHS 83 (Elm Hill Charter Oak x High Meadows Victoria) has produced a series of successful offspring. Defiance is a striking dark liver chestnut stallion standing 14.3 hands, bred by Stephen Herz and Christine Galineau of Windsor, New York, USA. Over the years he has become the second most versatile stallion produced in northern England, but his greatest success is as a show horse, being the breed's most successful in-hand stallion in Britain today. He bears a very close resemblance to his sire Elm Hill Charter Oak (Pecos x Bar-T Coredor), an extremely successful show horse in his lifetime and also very influential in the breeding programme of Monnington Morgans through a number of his daughters. Defiance possesses his sire's colour, characteristics, exuberant trot and animated attitude, a very eye-catching combination in the show ring. He is not only a consistent in-hand winner at the BMHS shows but is also very successful in open competition, having acquired a long list of in-hand stallion championship and reserve championship wins every year he has been shown, and with assorted handlers. In earlier years he had many performance wins with Kenneth Whitehead, under saddle and in driving classes, including Private Driving and FEI Combined Driving events, his driven dressage scores being quite outstanding. The Morgan's role as a Parade horse is still important amongst his local northern fans, and Defiance has often been asked to lead the parades to open the Kendal Harness Racing Events at the Kendal Raceway, receiving press coverage as 'one of the main attractions'. He was the first Morgan in Britain to receive sponsorship, from VW Trucks. Between 1982 and 1986 Defiance began to accumulate his in-hand successes and also participated in the Team displays at the Horse of the Year Show. After a few years of open performance competition in the north Defiance returned to the breed show ring when on lease to Lionhart Morgans of East Essex, owned by Sharon Hart, for the 1990 breeding season. The farm's trainer, Sarah Baker, took him to win the majority of BMHS stal-

111

Britain's top in-hand Morgan stallion, Hartland Defiance, here showing his ability between the shafts with Kenneth Whitehead.

112

lion in-hand classes and championships and also one held at a large East Essex Foreign Breeds show, thereby proving him a worthy contender yet again.

In 1991 he returned north to the stables of his new owner Ted Robson, with Kenneth Whitehead maintaining a keen interest in Defiance's progress. That same year Defiance achieved a major success at a north-eastern show by winning not only the Foreign Breeds class but also taking overall reserve show champion against Mountain and Moorlands, Dales and Welsh Cob class winners. In 1992, after experiencing his first season on the hunting field, Defiance encountered even stiffer competition in the Morgan show ring, but his dynamic appeal culminated in him taking the overall Grand Show Champion title and his yearling filly, Keepers Fancy Miss, out of Slect Passing Fancy, both owned by the Honorowski family, took overall Reserve Grand Show Champion at the Society's End of Year Championship Show held at Chester. His filly continued her success in 1993 and has proved herself unbeatable in in-hand youngstock classes in both breed and open competition, so far the only Morgan filly to achieve this.

Though Defiance is of average Morgan height he tends to contribute size to his offspring, plus his natural positivity, his 'twinkle' as Ted Robson describes it, and his athleticism. As a sire he is especially known for his tall son, the stallion Monnington Granados, who is so far the only Morgan in Britain to get to the top of its chosen

Monnington Granados, winner of the Concours d'Elegance at the Horse of the Year Show 1990, driven by Valerie Beckum. (*Photo courtesy Tessa Malcolm Brown*)

career in open competition by winning the Concours d'Elegance class at the Horse of the Year Show in 1990.

Scotland

Between 1979 and 1990 the development of the Morgan breed in Scotland appeared relatively encouraging, with a population averaging 11 Morgans, maintained at any one time by three small-scale breeders and one or two single horse owners.

However, to maintain American style show horses in Scotland poses various obstacles, such as finance, distance from appropriate shows and the effects of adverse weather conditions. Thus Scotland will undoubtedly remain one of the last sections of Britain to achieve a significant Morgan population and ownership.

Hardship, mainly due to world recession, has resulted in the loss of three out of four breeding farms, their stock sold to England and Europe. Although these losses were most unfortunate, Scottish owners and breeders have contributed to the overall development of the breed in Britain and other European countries by importing and producing quality and useful stock.

The first Scottish owner was Sue Buck of Helensburgh. Sue imported a yearling filly, Kinsman Cotton Queen, BMHS 41 (Applevale Kinsman x Dal Mor Cotton Candy), now owned by Landside Morgans, in 1979. Cotton became the inspiration behind Sue's untiring and dedicated efforts to promote the breed's versatility in Scotland almost single-handedly by organizing clinics, shows and demonstrations. Her most outstanding effort was the Gala of Western Horsemanship held in Glasgow in 1990. Scottish and English Morgans demonstrated Western riding, Saddleseat, dressage and Circus High School movements in hand. Other American breeds, the Quarter Horse and the Appaloosa, also demonstrated Western riding.

In 1990 Sue moved to the Scottish Morgan Horse Farm in Balgray, Ayrshire, with better facilities to enlarge her breeding programme and to hold events highlighting the development of Western ridden activities. She bought the proven broodmare, Littletown Flirt, from Belmont Morgans of Harrogate, Yorks. Flirt, a full sister to Monnington Andante, arrived in foal to the Belmont stallion, U.C. Echo, and produced a filly in 1991, who later was sold to Ireland. With five potential breeding mares Sue was preparing to become the most influential Morgan breeding and promotional enterprise in Scotland. Sadly by the end of 1991 the farm had to close for personal reasons and the horses were sold to an English owner.

Far north in Inverness-shire, Viewhill Morgans, owned by Mr Kiestra, began breeding Morgans in 1981. Mr Kiestra, originally from Holland, also bred Friesian horses. A small number of Morgan/Friesian foals were bred with interesting results, being somewhat similar to purebred stock. By 1988 Mr Kiestra stopped breeding Morgans and the majority of his purebred stock was sold to Sweden. In 1989 a new and promising farm was established by Anne and James Taylor near Dalry, Ayrshire. They purchased a British-bred yearling colt, Starwood Eclipse, BMHS 221 (Whippoorwill Osiris x Isail-Mor Starfire) who won practically every youngstock show he attended in Scotland. They also imported a stallion, Lone Pine Cajun, two in-foal mares and a filly from the USA to establish a new breeding programme, mainly for the production of sport horses. The Taylors choice of stock combined breed type, size and an abundance of proven versatility. By 1990 this farm too had closed, the horses sold south and the stallions later gelded. I became the only Scottish breeder, with little opportunity to improve the development of the Scottish Morgan by way of increasing its population.

I first became acquainted with Morgan horses as a child at equestrian summer camps in Ontario, Canada, in the 1960s. My first memories are of kind temperaments and humorous attitudes, and besides their pleasing rounded shape, strength and athleticism, it was this friendliness and inner gentleness that drew me to them. Many a moment was spent howling some awful misery into a Morgan mane, fortified by a nuzzle from an understanding Morgan nose. My family moved to Scotland in 1967, but in 1979, after spending three months working with Morgans in America, mainly with Anne Cole and her stallions in Vermont, I purchased a weanling colt, Monnington Andante, BMHS 38 (Ledgemere Alert x Novanna Ethan L). His arrival in Edinburgh in spring 1980 featured in the *Edinburgh Evening News*!

Andante, a dark chestnut, was the product of a breeding in the USA. His dam was imported in foal by Monnington Morgans in 1978. After five years of patient livery situations and ridden and driven training, we moved to Mountain Blow in 1985, a small hill-top farm in Lanarkshire and quickly learned what real wind and snow was and why all the trees were bent over to the east! That year Andante won Reserve Champion In-hand Morgan Stallion at his first breed show in Northumberland. He was invited to join the BMHS Team who were to perform at the Horse of the Year show, due to his Trojan horse appearance, but unfortunately we were unable to attend.

I never held plans to breed from Andante to any great extent, mainly because I thought we would always lack facilities. He initially remained a stallion due to his unique temperament and humorous individuality. However, as he matured it became evident that he had many excellent breed qualities to pass on to pure and part-bred stock. His northerly location has restricted purebred breeding but his use by artificial insemination has recently opened new doors and his first foal by this process was born in 1994. Andante has been siring part-bred stock since 1986 and purebred stock since 1988. His offspring are carrying on their sire's versatility in driving, dressage, Western, jumping and general family use.

On the home front Andante has sired foals every other year from the mare See Jay Melody (leased to us by Nancy Hedley-Dent and then gifted to us in 1994), who produced colts in 1988, 1990 and 1994 and a filly in 1992. Mt Top Manitou (1988), sold to Mrs Sheila Parrott, has been winning in novice and open Western performance classes, and Mt Top Boomeran (1990), sold to Mrs Kathe Randrup, has a future as a breed sire and performance horse in jumping and dressage. Kathe also bred twin colt foals by Andante out of the mare Rebelaire Satin when she was on lease from her owner, Ms Elizabeth Sharp, between 1990 and 1992.

Andante has not been heavily campaigned in the show ring but has done well in the dressage arena when competing at local level. In 1990 he performed the Dressage

Monnington Andante, Scotland's only Morgan stallion at the time of writing, showing a remarkable resemblance to the Justin Morgan statue at the University of Vermont. (*Photo by Francis Burton*)

The stallion Mt Top Boomeran, owned by Kathe Randrup.

Grand Finale at the Gala of Western Horsemanship in Glasgow, demonstrating lateral and extended work, ably ridden by Sarah Baker. An invaluable schoolmaster, Andante has assisted BHS students and both able-bodied and handicapped children. However, the majority of his life is spent enjoying such pursuits as dressage and jumping, roaming the Scottish forestry, herding sheep and harrowing the school. He is very much the family horse who enjoys switching on the 'power pack' when asked to do so.

9 The Morgan worldwide

Over the past 30 years or so equine activities have become increasingly popular, with greater promotion and diversity. Breeds native to specific countries, many of them recognized for specific uses, have increasingly gained popularity and organized international status.

The Morgan breed has benefited considerably from this new wave of opportunity. Its versatility and tractability are now appreciated the world over. Not all countries supporting the Morgan horse have formed clubs or national registers, but according to the AMHA list of Internationally Recognized Breed Clubs there are clubs in Canada, Britain, Italy, Spain, Germany, Sweden, Australia and more recently New Zealand.

Canada

Official development of the Morgan in Canada began much more recently than might first be supposed. Morgans are known to have been in the country since the early 1800s, but the majority of purebred stock was eventually outcrossed. Breed organizations did not begin forming until the 1950s, with the majority of clubs springing up in the 1960s. By 1992 the Canadian National Livestock Records revealed that 7,738 Morgans had been registered in the country.

The breed's national organization is the Canadian Morgan Horse Association Inc. (CMHA), based in Ludoc, Alberta, which maintains its own register under reciprocal agreement with the AMHA. Its structure and provision for senior and junior members and for the breed closely identify with those of the AMHA. There are nine associated clubs stretched across the vast line of provinces, from Nova Scotia in the east to British Columbia in the west, with British Columbia supporting two of the nine clubs.

Some provinces can boast of historic links with the very early Morgans and with a few individual horses that had significant influence on the breed's history in America.

American owners, breeders, trainers and judges have given and continue to give appreciable assistance to the breed's Canadian development by providing quality breeding and performance stock and by directly encouraging a wide range of social and competitive activities.

Canada is a sizeable part of the North American continent, consisting of 3,851,809 square miles of contrasting and awe-inspiring scenery, wildlife and climate, and huge expanses of sparsely populated territory. These conditions ensure that the breed's qualities of hardiness and adaptability continue.

The Canadians are very proud of their Morgans and are experiencing a healthy rate of growth, with useful breeding programmes and associated competitions, and successful incursions into the massive dominion of open competition. All aspects of the breed are supported and encouraged. The membership numbers of individual clubs are often small, some comparable to those of the larger European organizations. However, their achievements are considerable, especially when taking into account the number of miles that usually separate members from one another. Social events such as general get-togethers and fun horse days are very popular and are organized regularly.

It has been relatively easy for the Morgan to participate and develop in traditional Morgan-style show classes, as open competition already catered for many of these interests for other breeds. However, as the CMHA and its associated clubs have developed breed shows and classes of their own, including much needed in-hand classes, it is not uncommon to see Canadian licence plates heading for the Grand National Morgan Show held in Oklahoma each year. A healthy rivalry between the two countries is developing steadily.

In open competition Morgans are increasingly making a name for themselves as performers. One example is Nancy Beacon of Ontario and her Morgan Trijas Whiperpopper, who have been very successful in distance riding and endurance events. At the age of 21 in 1992, Whiperpopper had covered more competitive miles than any other horse of any breed in the country.

A second example, in Alberta, is W.A.W. Beau Heir, owned, trained and ridden by Trudy Narcott-Steele, who became the first registered Morgan to compete at Grand Prix level in dressage.

To prove the breed's capability as a competitive sport horse against other popular breeds, a Canadian-bred Morgan stallion, Foxtrim Classic, contributed to breed history by becoming the first Morgan to be accepted for enrolment in a European Style 100-Day Stallion Performance Test held in Keswick, Virginia in 1990. He completed

119

Foxtrim Classic, owned by Drs Wallace and Christina Jones of Sanquado, Alberta, pictured as a three year old.

the test with a very impressive overall score. Owned by Drs Wallace and Christina Jones of Sanquado, Alberta, Foxtrim Classic set a precedent for other Morgan stallions. (More detailed information on this topic is given in Chapter 10.)

Sweden

The Swedish Morgan Horse Association (SMHA) was the first society to be formed for Morgans on the European continent. Morgans have been in Sweden since 1972, but the SMHA was only formed in 1983. It supports over 100 members and a Morgan population of over 175, which is increasing fairly rapidly with a crop of 20 to 25 foals a year. The association maintains a purebred register but registration with the AMHA is also necessary.

A special stud book is maintained by the SMHA to record those mares and stallions licensed as approved breeding stock by the Swedish Horse Board, of which it is a well-known member in spite of being a small organization. Swedish law stipulates that any stallion that is likely to be used at stud has to pass a national evaluation test in order to be recognized. Swedish-bred stock are evaluated at the age of four, followed by tests of ability in riding as well as driving. Young stallions and any imported stallion entering and failing either of the tests will not receive a licence to stand at stud. Therefore it is necessary that very careful assessment is made of horses considered for importation.

An annual breed show is held by the association, usually inviting a judge from the USA. This show provides Morgan in-hand showing classes as well as performance classes, ridden and driven. However, Morgan shows and showing are not the primary concerns of Swedish owners, the main preference being to prove the performance capabilities of their horses in open competition.

In a salute to Sweden's most influential foundation Morgan stallion, Hanover Super Dan (1967–92), submitted to the *Morgan Horse Magazine* (December 1992), Olov Olofsson, President of the SMHA, states:

> It is probably safe to say that Super Dan and his Swedish offspring have made more of an example than Morgans from any other country to show sport people in Europe that the Morgan is a working horse. To prove this and to promote sound, typey and versatile horses with great stamina, we started to evaluate our breeding horses, both mares and stallions, in 1986.

The founding influence of the breed in Sweden is the Isaksbo Stuteri, a stud managed by Ove Stenson, who is a keen Morgan competitor and promoter. Isaksbo was founded in 1973 by the late Axel Johnson, a top businessman who lived part of his life in the USA. His daughter Antonia A. Johnson has carried on the stud's breeding programme since 1984 and for many years the Isaksbo horses have competed seriously in driving events. The offspring that the stud have sold have attained many competitive successes in dressage and jumping. Between 1972 and 1977 Johnson imported nine broodmares and one stallion, UVM Titan. Titan died in 1980 but according to Ove Stenson he left an Isaksbo-bred stallion – Isaksbo Donquijote (x

UVM Titan (*above*), Sweden's first Morgan stallion; and his offspring (*below*) Isaksbo Donquiejote with Isaksbo Elgirl competing in Finland, 1987. (*Photos courtesy Ove Stenson*)

Horseshoe's Lyncrest), foaled in 1978. Hanover Super Dan was found in America by Antonia in 1980 to replace Titan and was imported to become the stud's most influential breeding stallion.

Hanover Super Dan (Chasely Superman x Foxy's Easter Dawn) stood at 15.2 hands, and gained rapid popularity during his first few years in Sweden. He created so much interest in the breed that the SMHA was formed. Purchased primarily as a breeding stallion, it was felt that his talents were so great that he should not be 'hidden in a barn'. He was invited to display his ability at many big fairs and shows including the 1989 Dressage World Cup Finals held at the world-famous Gothenburg Horse Shoe, when he was 22 years old. At the age of 23 Super Dan led some of his offspring around the 1912 Olympic Arena at the 1990 Stockholm World Equestrian

SGS Ability (Hanover Super Dan x South Forty Maid). (*Photo courtesy Ove Stenson*)

Olov Olofsson with his purebred Lippitt mare, Madrona Trilby, pictured in 1988 as a three year old. (*Photo courtesy Mary Rein*)

Championships in front of thousands of spectators. His offspring have continued to prove their sire's worth in competition and as breeding stock. Super Dan sired a total of 63 offspring, 18 in America and 45 in Sweden. Four of his sons so far have passed all their evaluation tests.

However, this breeding success is not the final tribute to Super Dan, and Olov Olofsson ended his salute by saying:

> Hanover Super Dan is officially considered a first-class stallion among all Swedish breeds, and the Swedish Horse Board, who runs horse breeding in our country, will give him evaluation class ELITE, which is reserved for a very small number. Among one hundred carefully selected stallions of all breeds,

maybe one or two will be considered ELITE sires, and Hanover Super Dan is one of them. The Morgan world have just lost a horse to be proud of.

British-bred Morgans exported to Sweden have contributed to the Swedish promotion of the all-round Morgan sport horse. Bolbec Bonnibel (Pegasus Royal Pride x Rapidan Coquette) is perhaps the most well known. She was foaled in 1978, bred by Nancy Hedley-Dent of Northumberland, one of the BMHS founder members. Bonnibel, after a successful driving career in Britain, was sold at the age of nine to Margareta Sundberg of Stockholm. During her first year in Sweden Bonnibel placed first in dressage and jumping competitions and also lay sixth overall as Swedish Single Harness Horse in three-part competition under FEI rules. She has participated in breed displays and has had repeated success at the SMHA annual breed show, win-

Bolbec Bonnibel strides into a water hazard with her owner, Margareta Sundberg, driving.

125

ning the Morgan Sport Horse Association (USA) Trophy presented at the show for the Best Performance Morgan in Sweden.

Germany

In 1984 Ron Besler, a Morgan breeder from Alberta, Canada, realized the marketing potential of the breed in Germany, especially since leisure opportunities h increased for the German people in general. His German heritage and fluency in the language presented him with many advantages for his planned project. In 1985 Besler and a fellow breeder from Alberta, Eldon L. Bienert, took a three-year-old mare bred by Bienert to be exhibited and sold at the world-famous Equitana Fair in Essen, Germany, as the start of their promotions. The mare DVF Sweet Mystery, BMHS 161 (Treelane Mystery Man x Springfield Lady Fair) was to be an elusive proposition for Germany, as she was purchased by Dawn Sharif, an English owner and breeder, and taken home to Buckinghamshire.

Besler continued to export horses for sale at regular intervals, exhibiting them at the Fair. On one of these trips in 1989 he sold a mare to Hans Schilling, who has

The versatile mare Germany missed out on. DVF Sweet Mystery with Sara Sharif up. (*Photo by Pleasure Prints*)

become Germany's largest owner and most prolific breeder and breed promoter, establishing a farm at Rainrod before moving the bulk of his sales and breeding operations to Thueringen in former East Germany in 1990. By 1993 Schilling owned over 60 of the 90 Morgans in Germany, the others distributed between 16 recorded owners. Breed interest founded the International Morgan Horse Club of Germany (IMHC of Germany). There are two breed clubs in the country, the second being the sche Morgan Horse Association (DMHA), which was formed by seven breed enthusiasts and owners in Germany and Jill Jones of Montana, USA. The membership, who are very keen to maintain breed quality and characteristics, presently support 13 Morgans between them.

It is not mandatory for Morgan stallions to be licensed in Germany, but in a bid to ensure the breeding and performance potential of their horses members of the DMHA believe that breeding stallions should be evaluated and licensed.

Glamorgan Damien, AMHA 118344 (Glamorgan Noah x Glamorgan Augusta), a brown 15 hand stallion, was the first to be licensed. He was foaled in 1988 and bred by Dr Alden B. Starr of Syracuse, New York. His owner, Susan Fischer of Hamburg, West Germany, spent time with the Starr family while on a student exchange to Syracuse in 1988, becoming so attached to the colt that she returned home with him the following year. Damien is from a line of Morgans bred to be successful sport and carriage horses. He is a very athletic individual with superb balance and self-carriage. He competes in dressage, jumping, endurance and trail riding, and Western Reining events, and the intention is to add driving to his long list of achievements.

Equinox Black Hawk, AMHA 119097 (Courage of Equinox x Equinox Independence), a black stallion foaled in 1990 and bred by East of Equinox Farm Inc., of Manchester Centre, Vermont, is the second stallion to be licensed so far. He is owned by Sabine Franke of Iserlohn, a founder member of the DMHA. Glamorgan Damien is registered in the Rheinisches Pferdestammbuch, Bonn, Germany and Equinox Black Hawk in the Westfalisches (Westphalia) Pferdestammbuch, Munster, Germany. In the near future Schnuddel Mr Promise (Landside Mr Promise x Arduns Neva), foaled in 1990 and mentioned in the previous chapter, is to be put forward for licensing.

In Germany Morgans are predominantly used as pleasure mounts, ridden English and Western, with trail riding a very popular leisure activity. With the growth of Western riding (about 80 per cent of all Morgans in Germany are ridden Western) competitive classes including Cutting, Reining and Trail are also becoming very popular. Other competitive disciplines in which Morgans participate include dressage,

Equinox Black Hawk is the second Morgan stallion to be licensed for breeding in Germany.

jumping and endurance riding. Competitive Trekking, which combines trail, cross-country and long distance, is another popular sport which many people feel will become a highly competitive activity for Morgans. So far there is not a market for the traditional show Morgan, as the German people are unfamiliar with Park and Pleasure classes.

Italy

The development of the Morgan in Italy is still very much in its infancy, but news of the breed is steadily spreading through the country. The person behind the breed's

Hye Eire Figurine, owned by Roberto Aimone of Biella, shows excellent type and substance. She will be a good foundation mare for Italy.

initial promotion is Roberto Aimone of Biella. In 1987 Aimone purchased a stallion, Elm Hill Enchantor, and a mare, Hye Eire Figurine, who was imported in foal to an American stallion, Elm Hill Baystater. A few months later she produced a filly which Aimone named Beauty Baystater Gin.

These first three horses participated in demonstrations and exhibitions held by Aimone and attracted interest in the breed for pleasure riding. In 1992 Aimone imported a further six mares for resale. He was looking for typey mares who were already trained to saddle and would fulfil the pleasure riding purposes of his countrymen. The interest generated by Aimone has been enough to form a breed club, the Morgan Horse Club Italia.

10 The Morgan in sport

The inherent qualities of the Morgan and the performance capabilities developed over the years, together with its useful height range, have equipped the breed well to meet the challenges of today's sporting pursuits, for men, women and children alike.

In 1981 a new wave of publicity highlighted the breed's competitive ability, when a small group of North American Morgan horse owners and sport enthusiasts formed the Morgan Sport Horse Association (MSHA), 'to promote the idea of a North American bred horse for sport activities'. The MSHA supports a growing membership in North America, Great Britain, Sweden, Germany and France, maintaining what has become a far-reaching and significant influence in Morgan circles on both sides of the globe.

Since 1981 there has been a rapid increase in the number of Morgans active in competitive sport. Official breed literature has also increased its coverage and promotion of the 'Sport' Morgan. With more Morgan breeding and training programmes aimed at this sphere, the breed's marketing potential has improved overall, as more emphasis is placed on sound temperament, conformation and performance abilities.

The recent organization of an annual European-style 100-day Stallion Performance Test in North America, alternating between California (held by the International Sport Registry) and Virginia (through the American Hanoverian Association) has presented an ideal opportunity for individual Morgan stallions to prove their athleticism, stamina and temperament within the strict assessment of a

highly respected system. Though only a handful of Morgans to date have participated in these tests their results have highlighted the potential of the breed.

In 1989 the first Morgan to be accepted and enrolled in the 100-day Test held at November Hill Farm in Keswick, Virginia, was the black 15.2 hand stallion, Foxtrim Classic, then a four year old. Classic, owned and bred by two veterinarians, Drs Wallace and Christina Jones of Blue Fox Morgans in Sanguado, Alberta, Canada, was the smallest horse to complete the test, and he earned the respect of many people involved in the breeding of European Warmbloods and sport horses. He finished seventh in the company of ten top Hanoverian stallions, with an overall score of 91.9. The passing score for many Warmblood registries is 70, but the passing score required for licensing Hanoverian stallions, the most rigorously tested of the German breeds, is 90. Most impressive was Classic's index for the jumping phases: 108.48, ranking well above average in this area.

In 1991 two other Morgan stallions enrolled in the test in Virginia. Moorewood Excalibre, aged ten, and DJJJ Ebony Gold, aged six (again the smallest horses in the test at almost 16 hands), placed eleventh and fourth out of 15 horses, with scores of 82.22 and 106.36 respectively. Moorewood Excalibre received a reduced score because of his age.

In 1992 Funquest Erick, described as a remarkably strong and early maturing stallion, owned by Joyce Quigly of Lake City, Florida, became the second horse to be presented and honoured with the AMHA Sport Horse Award. However, Funquest

Foxtrim Classic (*left and below*) during the gait evaluation and the jumping phase at the November Hill Farm Test, 1989. (*Photos courtesy Wallace and Christina Jones*)

Erick's achievement was unusual as he began accumulating the necessary points to win five Bronze Medallions, out of the six divisions offered, as a two year old in 1989.

He won a Bronze Medallion in the Hunter–Jumper division of the AMHA Open Competition Programme. His owner received criticism for jumping him so young but she maintained that Erick had been properly conditioned, had the bone and potential and an exceptional mental attitude, and that if he had soured or resisted in any way she would have stopped immediately. In 1990 Erick attained his Bronze Medallions in First Level Dressage and in driving. That year, due to a freak accident, he sustained devastating injury to a foreleg and underwent a six-hour operation with little hope of an eventual recovery to soundness. Remarkably by the end of the year Erick was healed and sound, and after considerable thought Joyce decided to continue campaigning for the Sport Horse Award by spring 1991.

They attended competitive trail riding and combined training events in many different states, attaining their remaining Bronze Medallions. Erick has attracted a lot of interest, especially from competitive trail breeders. Due to his astounding success he was invited by the President of the American Warmblood Society to join their registry as an official papered American Warmblood Society Stallion. In an article highlighting Erick (*The Morgan Horse*, June 1992), Betsy Viets wrote:

> With stallions like Funquest Erick influencing the breeding of future American Warmbloods and adding Morgan blood to competitive trail horses, the tentacles of the breed are reaching into all areas of equine activity.

In North America there is a supportive approach to promotion and provision of competitive activities for horses. Within this structure, breed organizations are complemented by Service Clubs which cater for specific activities, and such is the case with the Morgan. This gives breeds the opportunity to compete within their own dominions. However, open competition adds a whole new dimension, and here the Morgan has benefited, gaining increased recognition, respect and demand, not only for its versatility but also for its ability to specialize for selected goals.

The skills that were, and still are, used on the Western range are brought together in Western ridden competitive events in many countries around the world today. The Western Reining and Stock Horse needs a high degree of technical skill and mental discipline. The horses must have a natural balance, a strength of conformation and a strong supporting musculature to be capable of tight pivot turns, sliding stops and

Hawk's Nest Capri owned by Betty Welles of Connecticut, ridden by Luck Snook. By 1991 Capri had accumulated 2000 competitive miles, winning most major events and 100 mile rides.

133

quick surges of speed. An honest and willing disposition with a large amount of intelligence and aptitude to learn quickly is also very important. Competitive Western Reining has become popular throughout the world. In North America an increasing number of professional trainers are experiencing the Morgan's natural aptitude and ability in this field, many stating that the Morgan is a good candidate and should receive greater encouragement for Reining within its own breed events as well as in open competition. A fine representative of the Western ridden Morgan in North America is Mont Francis Claire, owned by Barbara and Steve Elfers of Vacaville,

Mont Francis Claire showing the necessary skill, power and calm required of a good Reining horse. Note the facial expression. (*Photo by Caroline Fyffe Photography*)

California. Claire began her competitive career in 1989, quickly becoming a top contender in open competition in 1991 and also becoming the National Morgan Cutting and Stock Horse Association High Point Reining Champion.

Western riding in Europe is gaining a foothold, especially in Germany and Britain,

Monnington Gershwin, Western Pleasure champion at the Belmont All Morgan Show, 1990. Anna Fisher up. (*Photo courtesy Anna and Richard Fisher*)

as more people appreciate the specific skills involved and the trust that must exist between horse and rider. In Britain Western riding is promoted mainly by the Western Equestrian Society (WES) and the Western Horseman's Association. The American Quarter Horse, for obvious reasons, has been the mount predominantly chosen by Western devotees.

In more recent years Morgans have been edging their way into British Western equestrian events. Monnington Jubilate (as described in Chapter 7) was the first British Morgan to achieve success as early as 1986. Between 1986 and 1991 Morgans have mainly appeared ridden Western in displays and in Western Pleasure classes at BMHS and local shows, but in 1992 two four-year-old Morgans brought renewed interest to the breed and its natural ability in this field.

Picture Perfect (Valiant Tony x Sorene), a bay stallion, jointly owned by the Pamphilon family and his rider/trainer Caroline Lockhart of Kent, made their debut at Novice level in Western Pleasure, Horsemanship and Trail classes. Their greatest accomplishment of the year was to receive a Supreme Championship win in the WES classes held at the Malvern August Show.

Mt Top Manitou (Monnington Andante x See Jay Melody), a gelding, was purchased as a weanling by Shelia Parrott of Suffolk who believed that Manitou would make an excellent Reining horse. Her beliefs were well founded, and in 1992 Manitou, expertly trained and ridden by Sheila Whelan of Malvern, Worcester, won an astounding 29 out of 48 classes entered, which included Western Pleasure, Horsemanship, Trail and Reining at Novice and Open levels, making him the WES High Point Champion that year, and also the Most Improved Young Horse of the Season. Both these young Morgans are pursuing more advanced training programmes.

Within the last 20 years or so three highly competitive fields that have seen an expansion of Morgan participation are dressage, jumping, and combined training (eventing), with its three phases of show jumping, cross-country jumping and dressage. In the past the breed's progress in these spheres was hindered by a lack of promotional support and the Morgan's smaller size and characteristic movement, when compared to those of other breeds, already recognized for their size and practical abilities. However, the breed's definitive success in open dressage competition has meant that some North American Morgan shows plan to expand their dressage divisions to attract more entrants.

Though some are surprised at the breed's achievements in dressage, perhaps not confident of its ability to maintain the required length of stride and suppleness

Mt Top Manitou looking towards a successful future with his trainer/rider Sheila Whelan. (*Photo by Ruth Dwornik, courtesy Sheila Parrott*)

through the top-line, Morgans become very good candidates when correct suppling and softening exercises are used together with an attitude of request, not demand. The advantages the breed has are that the set of the neck into the shoulders makes collected work easier.

A prime example of the success the Morgan can achieve is provided by Big Bend Doc Davis, a 15.2 hand stallion jointly owned by his rider, Mona Sansoucy-Gaudet, and Catherine Sansoucy of Grosvenordale, Connecticut. Retired at the age of 17 in

1992, Big Bend Doc Davis competed seriously during the 1980s and became the first Morgan stallion to compete at Grand Prix level, and the first winner of the AMHA Gold Medal for outstanding achievement in open competition. In 1991 some of the first place winners of the All-Breed Morgan Award Programme were Brown's Fiddle Dee, owned by Deborah Guylay of Pennsylvania (Fourth Level and Prix St George), and Ten Penny Action, owned by Janet Moulding of Massachusetts (Intermediate 1). These horses and riders have continued to progress and many new young horses are proving themselves as up and coming prospects.

In France, Morgans are actively being bred for dressage and in Britain, though no one has yet campaigned seriously enough to compete a Morgan in national competition, there are many Morgans attaining consistent success at local events from Preliminary to Medium levels.

One North American farm that has greatly influenced the promotion of Morgans as sport horses is Taproot Farm of Hinesburg, Vermont, owned by Charles and Charlotte Ross. With their daughter, Jackie, and later her husband Ben Qua, Taproot horses have been successfully campaigned in the show ring, in breed performance and open competition in a remarkable assortment of disciplines, some of which are: (driving) Roadster, open driving – singles, pairs, tandem, unicorn and four in-hand; (riding) dressage, distance and endurance and, not least, combined training.

Jackie Ross Qua began eventing on the farm's foundation mare, UVM Harmony, in 1966. She was active in the Pony Club, ignoring outside advice to swap on to Thoroughbred mounts. Over the years the Ross's views have reflected those of other competitors who have found the Morgan to have great heart, soundness and staying power and a love of jumping. Statistics show that the number of Morgans is shooting up in both the United States Dressage Federation (USDF) and the United States Combined Training Association (USCTA).

In an article 'A Good Go – Morgans Making It In Combined Training' by Stephanie Lile (*The Morgan Horse*, November 1991), under the heading 'Throw your heart over first and the rest will follow', is written the words of encouragement which eventing enthusiasts may find useful:

In the Morgan breed's early history, its excellence was extolled by its versatility, strength, stamina and HEART. Today while the demands placed on the breed have changed, these characteristics are gradually being recognized – and prized – by members of the combined training world. The combination of agility, over-land endurance, and calmness once applied to a variety of home-

Big Bend Doc Davis (*above*) ridden by Mona Sansoucy-Gaudet, 1988; (*below*) Brown's Fiddle Dee ridden by Deborah Guylay at the 1987 American Horse Show Association finals, Temple Farms. (*Photo by Margaret Kaiser*)

stead chores and later remount services, has, in its way, resurfaced in the demands of combined training.

The article goes on to discuss the 'size issue' and suggests that the breed is not at a disadvantage when compared to some top event horses, such as Mark Todd's 15.3 hand eventer Charisma. The pair twice won the Olympic Gold Medal in the Three-Day Event, 'and both Poltroon and Marcus Aurelius, each horse measuring just a touch over 15 hands, were phenomenal international competitors'.

The general view of those interviewed for the article was that 'What a horse lacks in size, it seems his "heart" can make up for', and that 'as the Morgan finds its way into the Pony Clubs across the country [North America] young riders and their instructors are beginning to find value in the Morgan's size and temperament'.

In Britain more and more Morgan horses are joining the competitive show jumping and eventing worlds with both junior and senior riders. In other European countries such as Sweden, where Morgans are not imported or bred for careers as show horses, jumping and eventing is well supported.

Taproot Command Pilot jumping for joy and making it look easy. In training with Denny Emerson of the US Combined Training Association. (*Photo courtesy Mr and Mrs C. Ross*)

The Combined Driving Event (CDE) – consisting of three phases: dressage, obstacles (cones) and hazards (marathon), a driven form of eventing – is the toughest competitive test a driving horse can experience. Combined driving is becoming increasingly popular worldwide and Morgans are competing extremely successfully in national and international competition.

Sherry Ackerman Ballou of Maranatha Training Stables, Brookfield, Vermont, USA, provides us with some useful information on the preparation of the Morgan for this sport and for endurance and distance work in general. The stable prepares all breeds of horses for competition in 'The Three D's . . . Driving, Dressage and Distance'.

We have found the Morgan horse to be very brave and unflappable, rendering them very useful in the hazard section of CDE marathons. They are also capable of maintaining a brisk trot over rough terrain for long distances without undue fatigue. They do not have the phenomenal Pulse/Respiration recovery of the Arabian breed but properly conditioned (and this is the key!) they will

Otter Brook Alida and Green Acres Debbie driven in tandem by Peter Morin. (*Photo by Sterling Stephenson, courtesy Jennifer DuBois*)

always be able to maintain stamina, strength and speed on marathon and/or long distance. The key to winning in endurance/distance driving with a Morgan is to calibrate the conditioning programme to specific Morgan parameters, rather than to adopt generic procedures that are generally developed with Arabians in mind.

The Morgan's capacity for cardiovascular performance has to be built very slowly, over an extended period of time, with special emphasis on respiratory recoveries. It is not unusual to see the hazard times of Morgans to be consistently faster than those times put in by other breeds. Many Morgans depend upon their strength on marathon day to pull themselves up a placing or two in the overall standings. I have seen drivers such as Spencer Kipe (New Jersey), W. Charles Ballou (Vermont), and Bill Orth (New Jersey) move up as many as four placings after an especially fast and accurate marathon with Morgan horses.

Ranatha Stanhope, a 13.3 hand Morgan mare competing very successfully in Single Pony divisions. Driven by W. Charles Ballou, seen here negotiating the cones at a Combined Driving Event. (*Photo courtesy Charles and Sherry Ballou*)

In 1989–90 Maranatha Stables pioneered the concept of eventing the smaller (under 14.2 hand) Morgan horse in Combined Driving Events in the Pony Division. They chose Ranatha Stanhope, a 13.3 hand Morgan, owned by Alice Thiele of Annadale, New Jersey. Driven by W. Charles Ballou she was overwhelmingly successful in the Preliminary Single Pony Divisions and was competed in Advanced Single Pony Divisions in 1991, the first time in history that a Morgan was shown in this division, generally dominated by Welsh and Arabian/Welsh crosses. In 1992 Ranatha Stanhope placed first Intermediate Single Pony at the Myopia CDE in Massachusetts and was Champion driven distance horse at three separate events.

The pinnacle of any sport is to be given the opportunity to compete at international level. Combined Driving has, so far, seen the greatest Morgan participation and challenges in international competition. The famous father and son pair, Kennebec Count

Broadwall Paradeson competing at the Royal Windsor Horse Show, driven by Meg Ferguson. (*Photo by Ronni Nienstedt, courtesy Meg Ferguson*)

143

and Kennebec Russel, owned by Margaret Gardiner of South Woolwich, Maine, were twice on the US Equestrian Team, representing the USA at Sandringham, England in 1985 and at Rosenbeck, Germany in 1987. Meg Ferguson of Greeve, Rhode Island, drove her Broadwall Paradeson with the US Team at the Royal Windsor Horse Show in 1990, and despite finding the water hazard deep for her 14.3 hand stallion, placed third amidst 12 top singles in the Harrod's International Grand Prix. The Team placed fourth overall.

Bill Orth of Stockton, New Jersey, as a member of the US Team, competed for the Master's Trophy at the Royal Windsor Horse Show in 1989. The Master's Trophy is a challenge trophy presented by Harrod's, the prestigious English department store, to commemorate the 10th Duke of Beaufort's presidency of the Royal Windsor Horse Show (1944–84). It is awarded to a group of three representing a single nation and consisting of one four in-hand, one pair and one single horse. Also in 1989 Bill Orth, the single driver for the American Team, with his gelding New Ran's Hawk, was the first American Single to compete in this International Driving Trial. He claimed an impressive second place.

On 17 May 1992 Orth returned to Windsor with his 13-year-old gelding accompanied by another single driver and Morgan owner, George Hoffman, also of New Jersey. Hoffman, who had competed against Orth for some time driving other breeds, decided, like a number of other drivers in the Single Division, that the only way to beat him was by having a Morgan too. He bought and campaigned Morgan Woods Yankee.

Orth and Hoffman placed first and second respectively in the Single Horse Division of the Harrod's Internationl Grand Prix competition. Orth was also a member of the American Team, which turned in a combined score of 269.6 (the least total of combined penalty points), bringing the United States the coveted Master's Trophy.

All the American whips went on to compete in Scotland at the St Fort Driving Trials held the week following Windsor. The temperature drop in the north had little effect and Orth and his gelding won the Strutt and Parker Challenge Trophy for the Open Single Horse Champion. Orth also won the Maxwell Perpetual Trophy for the Best Driver Over Sixty and later remarked with some amusement: 'The sting of the "Over 60" was removed when I looked at the trophy and read the name of the first recipient in 1983: "His Royal Highness the Duke of Edinburgh".'

The Duke of Edinburgh has himself recognized the value of Morgans for Combined Driving. In the second edition of his book *Competition Carriage Driving*,

New Ran's Hawk leaving the water hazard on the marathon at Windsor, 1989, Bill Orth driving. (*Photo by Alf Baker, courtesy Bill Orth*)

he states about the breed: 'these strong, active and very fast trotters have proved to be well-suited to driving competitions'. Morgans in Britain are generally receiving increased respect in this sphere. In FEI Combined Driving, three Morgans in particular have been making excellent progress with their owners in recent years, all members of the Midlands Driving Trials Group. They are Monnington Gershwin, Monnington Gamba and Pennington Harlem.

Monnington Gershwin, BMHS 166 (Tarryall Gene Thiery x Saddleback Silhouette), an eight-year-old stallion owned by Anna and Richard Fisher of Sheffield, has been very competitively campaigned over the last few years, driven by Richard Fisher. In 1992 he placed third on the Midlands Group League Tables for the Jill Neill Trophy (Open Horse and Open Pony) with a score of 29, three points below the top score, out of 74 competitors. The mare Monnington Gamba, BMHS 172 (Tarryall Gene Thiery x Panorama Pavane) is owned by Pat Prenton, also of

Anna and Richard Fisher competing with their stallion Monnington Gershwin, through the water hazard. (*Photo courtesy A. and R. Fisher*)

Sheffield, and placed twenty-sixth in the same competition with a score of 11 points, recording an excellent result for her first full open competitive season taken at a steady pace. Barbara James of Derbyshire and her gelding Pennington Harlem, BMHS 175 (Robbins Night Flight x Monnington Aria), also had a successful season in 1992, placing fourteenth out of 55 competitors competing for the Weston Trophy for Best Overall Novice Horse and Pony. Interestingly all three horses have several things in common. They all participate with the Midlands Driving Trials Group, carry the blood of one of Britain's most influential Morgan sires, either first or second generation, and were foaled in 1985. It must have been a very good year!

Due to the breed's inherent suitability as a harness horse, whether for sport or show, it is not surprising to learn that it is in competitive driving that the Morgan in Britain has achieved its greatest success. Not only has the Morgan proved itself worthy against many other breeds and types in the demanding world of sport, it has appealed to the eye of judges looking for an overall balanced picture of motion, physical beauty and temperament. In Private Drive and Concours d'Elegance the Morgan has become a strong contender at all levels, especially with Tessa Malcolm Brown and her Company Sealmaster Draught and Weatherseals of Cambridge, leading the field with outstanding success.

Sealmaster first became associated with the breed in 1987 when Tessa Malcolm Brown purchased the stallion Eaglhead Regal Heir, BMHS 87 (Tarryall Gene Thiery x Monnington Jubilate), to pursue her driving interests. One Morgan has led to others – quite a team, in fact. The second Morgan to arrive in the yard was Monnington Granados, BMHS 171 (Hartland Defiance x Hever Sequoia), a liver chestnut stallion standing nearly 16 hands, purchased from Monnington Morgans in the late 1980s. Within a very short time Granados became the first Morgan in Britain to win an Open Drive Championship and World Breeds Drive. These successes were a wonderful individual achievement and also promotion for the breed, but in 1990 they were surpassed when, besides becoming the first Morgan to qualify for the Concours d'Elegance final at Britain's most prestigious show, the Horse of the Year Show, Granados, driven by Valerie Beckum, won the class and earned the title of Concours d'Elegance Horse of the Year 1990. He went on to qualify again the following year, a real achievement as only 12 turnouts can qualify from over 400 entries.

In 1992 two more Sealmaster horses qualified, Monnington Conductor, BMHS 77 (Tarryall Gene Thiery x Springervale Kristen), driven by Heidi Eagle, and a recently imported gelding, Thankyou Ovation (Sugar Run Ovation x Thankyou Dearly), driven by Tessa Malcolm Brown. That same year Conductor qualified for the

147

National Carriage Driving Championships and came third in the semi-final. He has also been an Open Private Drive Champion and a Reserve Private Drive Champion (BDS) in Scotland. Monnington Descant, BMHS 95 (Monnington Motif x Tarryall Cadenza) also qualified for the National Carriage Driving Championships in 1992 and again in 1993, and is a past Novice Champion Private Drive (BDS Scotland) and winner of the World Breeds Private Drive (BDS Scotland) in 1992 and 1993.

With regard to the National Carriage Driving Championships, Private Drive is divided into sections by vehicle description and/or type or breed of horse or pony: i.e. Hackney, Registered Welsh, Mountain and Moorland etc. Morgans would come under non-Hackney type to a Gig or a Country Vehicle etc., and also Pairs (all breeds). The Championships are held in Windsor Great Park, and out of the semi-

Monnington Granados, Concours d'Elegance Horse of the Year 1990.

148

The two brothers Thankyou Ovation and Thankyou Oh Wow (Sugar Run Ovation and Thankyou Dearly) driven by Mrs Tessa Malcolm Brown. (*Photos by Event Print 'M', courtesy Tessa Malcolm Brown*)

final classes the first and second only go through to the finals which are judged by a panel of judges awarding points for each horse or pony.

Sealmaster Draught and Weatherseals are proud to have such a high profile in Morgan horse promotion and show fearlessly under all judges and against all comers. Their horses have been regularly shown at breed shows with consistent success. In open competition, such as Private Drive classes against other breeds including Welsh Cobs, Hackneys (and various crosses), Mountain and Moorland, Dutch Gelderlanders and Friesians, the Morgan is judged more competitively and receives wider publicity in every aspect. In recent years both Conductor and Granados have also had success in sidesaddle classes.

In 1993 four Sealmaster Morgans qualified for the Concours d'Elegance final at the Horse of the Year Show: Monnington Conductor (Heidi Eagle, driver), Monnington Descant (Valerie Beckum, driver), Outrageous (Supreme Command x Gladgay's Katy M), imported as a stallion but later gelded, and Thankyou Ovation. Both geldings were driven by Tessa Malcolm Brown in separate qualifiers so only one could go on to compete in the final. It seems that Sealmaster are the first yard in history to qualify four horses in the same year for this select class of 12 qualifying entries, a remarkable achievement for the Morgan breed and all concerned.

11 Conclusion

For the first 100 years of the Morgan's existence there was no official breed organization. The survival of the Morgan was entirely dependent upon its characteristic and resourceful ability to thrive in varied climates and environments and to adapt to various requirements and fashionable trends. As a result of this adaptability, other advantages were realized, mainly that the breed was used to upgrade existing types and newly developing breeds. For some breed enthusiasts this was a distinct disadvantage. Obviously much is owed to those individuals who sought to preserve the breed, especially through its times of decline, though in truth there was a distinct conflict of opinion amongst them as to what made a Morgan a Morgan.

Basically two factions emerged which caused rancour and controversy for many years. The basis of their differences related to the retention of maximum blood purity within the breed versus using semi-related or even unrelated outcrosses to suit individual interpretation and popular demand.

The Morgan found official recognition in 1894 with the publication of its first breed Register. However, here too it was felt that little was done, through the rules of registration, to deter outcrossed stock from being admitted to the Register, until 1948 when a new governing rule came into force prohibiting the registration of progeny bred from unregistered stock. Even though the two factions still exist in milder form today, breed type, performance and character prevail, a remarkable achievement for any breed that evolved from a 'homespun' background as did the Morgan horse.

It is apparent that no other horse breed will again emerge and survive such a mixture of influences as there have been on the Morgan. The key to his survival and his continued versatility and success is his breed type, a description which has been bandied about by those closely associated with the breed for years.

For those less familiar with the Morgan, it is hard to put a finger on what this emotive word 'type' really means. This is because Morgan type is not just a physical thing. The Morgan's individual presence, his gentle vibrancy, and what can only be described as his humour are characteristics which ooze from his pores, a visible charisma of his inner self. This is what makes a Morgan a Morgan. This persistence of character is what initially attracts people to the breed and invites them to further discovery. From a light-hearted point of view this unique characteristic, surviving 200 years of change, makes them ideal for the adventurer, the pioneering spirit, the 'finger-dipper taster', who provides variety and human contact to the Morgan. This is opposed to the 'feed-em and leave-em' attitude often exhibited by the 'pet-horse' owner. The Morgan's sense of humour combined with his innate brand of intelligence compared to many breeds is the difference between French 'Haute cuisine' and hospital food.

In short, the Morgan thrives on any activity, and is a staunch individualist which both offers and desires an affectionate and communicative relationship.

Bibliography

Acton, Lord, *The Cambridge Modern History, The United States* (Cambridge University Press, 1903)

AMHA (American Morgan Horse Association) *The Morgan Horse Magazine,* numerous monthly issues (1955–1993)

American Morgan Horse Institute, *The Morgan Horse Judging Standards* (1993)

American Morgan Horse Registry, Volumes IV to XIII

Battell, Joseph, *The Morgan Horse and Register*, Volume I (1894), Volume II (1905)

BMHS (British Morgan Horse Society) Newsletters and Magazines (1978–1993)

Childs, Marilyn Carlson, *Riding Show Horses* (Arco, 1972)

Childs, Marilyn Carlson, *The Men Behind the Morgan Horse* (1979)

Cook, O. W., 'Sire of Justin Morgan', *Wallace's Monthly* (Feb. 1879)

Cook, O. W., 'Dutch Horses', *Wallace's Monthly* (July 1879)

Crowell, Pers, *Cavalcade of American Horses* (McGraw Hill, 1951)

HRH Duke of Edinburgh, *Competition Carriage Driving*, 2nd edition (J. A. Allen, 1994)

Farshler, Earl R., *American Saddle Horse* (1934)

Flint, C. L., *The Horses of New England*, US Department of Agriculture Report (c. 1870)

Gianoli, Luigi, *Horse and Man*, English translation (George Unwin, 1969)

Hall, Ruth, *A Few Words on Horses*, US Department of Agriculture Report (c. 1870)

Henry, Marguerite, *Justin Morgan had a Horse* (Checkerboard Press, 1954)

Jett-Pittenger, Peggy, *Morgan Horses* (A. S. Barnes, 1967)

Leonard, W. L. 'The Blood of Justin Morgan', *Wallace's Monthly* (Sept. 1879)

Leonard, W. L. 'The Pedigree of Justin Morgan', *Wallace's Monthly* (June 1879)

Lile, Stephanie, 'A Good Go – Morgans Making it in Combined Training', *The Morgan Horse Magazine* (November 1991)

Linsley, Daniel C., *Morgan Horses* (1857)

Loch, Sylvia, *The Royal Horse of Europe* (J. A. Allen, 1986)

McLuhan, T. C. *Touch the Earth: A Self Portrait of Indian Existence* (Abacus, 1973)

Mellin, Jeanne, *The Complete Morgan Horse* (Stephen Green Press, 1986)

Morgan, Robert, *The Morgan Horse of the West* (Vantage Press, 1987)

Middlebury College, *The Morgan Horse and Register*, Volume III (1915)

Owen, Mabel, 'Justin Morgan 1', *The Morgan Horse Magazine* (August 1962)

Perlee, Gail, 'Western Working Family of Morgans: An Overview', *Arizona Morgan Horse Association Magazine* (1991)

Reese, H. H. *Breeding Morgan Horses*, US Department of Agriculture Circular 199 (c. 1927)

Rommel, George M., *The Regeneration of the Morgan Horse*, US Bureau of Animal Industry Circular 163 (1910)

Ryder, Tom, *The High Stepper* (J. A. Allen, 1961)

Spencer, Sally, *The Directory of Morgan Horses in Great Britain* (privately published, 1988)

Sumner, Dayton, 'The Mare who Made Bennington Famous', *The Morgan Horse Magazine* (July 1990)

Telford, Kenneth A., *Lippitt Register*, 2nd edition (privately published, 1986)

Telford, Kenneth A., *The Origins of the Modern Morgan: A Study in Contrasts* (privately published, 1988)

Winkler, Marshall N., 'A New Look at an Old Family', *The Morgan Horse Magazine* (July 1966)

Index of horses' names

Page numbers in italics refer to illustrations.

Abbott, 61
Abonette, 61
Agazizz, 50, 59
Allandorf, 69
Allen F1, 69
Allen Franklin, 50
Allen King, 50, 55
Andon Vigil Charlie, 107
Anneigh Dark Cloud, 109
Applevale Cadence, 81, 86, 95
Applevale Kinsman, 107, 114
Arduns Neva, 109–10, 125
Artemisia, 29–30, 34, 40
Ashbrook, 40–2
Audrey, 33

Bald Mt Black Cloud, 96
Bald Mt Pansy, 107
Ballad of Goshen, 81
Bar-T Coredor, 111
Beamington, 58
Beautiful Bay, 3
Beauty Baystater Gin, 129
Bell Marea, *39*
Belle Meade, 62
Belmont Fantasy, 100
Ben Franklin, 49
Bennington, 29–30, 33, 40, 45
Big Bend Doc Davis, 137–8, *139*
Bilirubin, 38
Bill Bailey, 62
Billie, 29
Bird Pepper, 59
Black Hawk, 13, 69
Blood Chief, 68
Blood's Black Hawk, 68

Bob B, 38
Bob Morgan, 59
Bolbec Arpeggio, 85
Bolbec Bonnibel, 85–6, 110, 125–6
Bolbec Diva, 94
Bolbec Prima, 84
Bonnie A, 55
Bonnie Jean, 38
Bradford's Telegraph, 69
Bridget, 38, 40
Broadwall Drum Major, 57
Broadwall Paradeson, *143*, 144
Broadwall Phyldon, 81
Brown's Fiddle Dee, 138, *139*
Bulrush, 7, 12, 15–16
Byerley Turk, 9

Cabell's Lexington, 29, 68
Calcutt Elms Tornado, 100, *101*
Canfield, 32, 59
Carolyn, 33
Casey Tibbs, 107
Charlie, 51
Chasely Superman, 123
Chetco, 49
Chief Bugler, 59
Chingadero, 99
Chocolate, 57
Congo, 50
Copperbottom (Canadian), 70
Cornwallis, 47, 57, 58, 95, 96
Country Dusty Lady, 107
Country March Squire, 107
Courage of Equinox, 127
Croydon Mary, 38, 42

Croydon Prince, 15, 38, 40
Cynthia, 62

Dainty Dot, 81
Daisette, 49
Daisy Knox, 55
Dal-Mor Cotton Candy, 107, 114
Damascus, 61
Daniel Lambert, 49
Darley Arabian, 9
Deer Run Command, 102
Denning Allen, 28
Devon Dusty, 107
Devon Hawk, 57
Diamond, 3
DJJJ Ebony Gold, 131
Dolly Spanker, 69
Domino Vermont, 55
Donald, 9, 38
Dorthea Allen, 104
Dude, 9
Dunoir Laddie, *98*
Dunoir Montana, 97–9
DVF Sweet Mystery, 126
Dyberry Robin, *46*

Eaglhead Regal Heir, 147
Easter Vermont, 55
Eaton Horse, 68
Ecstasy, 62
Elmhill Baystater, 129
Elmhill Charter Oak, 111
Elmhill Enchantor, 128
Emerald's Top Lady, 100
Emily, 38, 40
Envi's Doris, *46*

155

Equinox Black Hawk, 127, *128*
Equinox Independence, 127
Ethan Allen 50, 13, 28, 69
Ethan Allen 2nd, 15, 36, 54
Ethan Allen 3rd, 15
Evelyn, 38

Fanita, 59
Fannie 2nd, 59
Fanny Scott, 28
Fearnaught, 16
Figure, 1, Chapter 1 *passim*; *see also* Justin Morgan
Fleetfield, 59
Florette, 50, 59
Flyhawk, 50, 59, 62, 105
Flying Jubilee, 62
Folly, 50
Foxtrim Classic, 119, *130*, 131
Funquest Erick, 131–2

Gala Girl, 59
Gayflower, 62
Gaymaid of Wenloch, 62
Gayselba, 62
Gemini Sapphire, 100, 105, 106
General Gates, 9, 26, 28–9, 57
George Wilkes, 69
Gifford Morgan, 14, 16, 69
Ginger Vermont, 55
Gladgays Katy M, 150
Glamorgan Augusta, 127
Glamorgan Clivia, 111
Glamorgan Damien, 127
Glamorgan Noah, 127
Glenns Phoenix, 107
Godolphin Arabian, 9, 70
Go Hawk, 50, 59
Green Acres Debbie, *141*
Green Mountain Morgan, *see* Hale's Green Mountain
Gringo, 62

Hale's Green Mountain, 15, 36, *37*
Hambletonian, 69
Hannah, 38
Hanover Super Charger, 84
Hanover Super Dan, 121, 123–5
Harrison Chief, 29
Hartland Defiance, 111, *112*, 147
Hawk Jim, 57
Hawk's Nest Capri, *133*
H-Bar Panama, 97, *98*, 99
H. C. Mays Reflection, 101
Headlight Morgan, 15, 54, 55, 57, 61, 70
Helenfield, 55
Helen Mala, 55
Helen May, 55
Hemala, 55
Hepatica, 47
Heroda, 59
Hever Sequoia, 147
Highmeadows Victoria, 111
Hippolyta, 38, 40
Homestake, 55
Horseshoes Lyncrest, 123
Hye Eire Figurine, 128, *129*

Indian Chief, 68
Isail-Mor Starfire, 115
Isaksbo Donquiejote, 121–3
Isaksbo Elgirl, *122*

Janee, 96
Joe Baily, 55
John A. Darling, 40
Juban, 50
Jubilee de Jarnette, 49, 59
Jubilee King, *49*, 50, 55, 57, 59, 62, 96, 105
Jubilee Lambert, 50
Jumina, 59, 62
Just-A-Nod Exodus, 100
Justin Morgan, 1, 2, *5*, 8, 17, 18, 19, *27*, 36, 57, *60*, 68, 69, 70; *see also* Figure
Juzan, 50

Keepers Fancy Miss, 113
Ken Carmen, 59
Kennebec Count, 55, *56*, 143
Kennebec Russel, 55, *56*, 144
Keomah Laurie L, 100
King de Jarnette, 59
Kinsman Cotton Queen, 107, 114
Kitty B, 55
Klyona, 61

Lady de Jarnette, 50
Lady Spar, 57
Lady Stratton, 54
Landside Flirt, 110
Landside Masterpiece, *107*
Landside Mr Promise, 107, *108*, 110, 125
Landside Music Man, 108
Ledgemere Alert, 100, 115
Linsley, 57
Linspar, 57
Lippitt Byfield, 42
Lippitt Ethan Ash, 42, 43
Lippitt Kate Moro, 40, 42
Lippitt Mandate, 42
Lippitt Morman, 42
Lippitt Moro, 42
Lippitt Moro Ash, *42*
Lippitt Nekoman, 42
Lippitt Pecos, 46
Lippitt Rob Roy, *41*
Lippitt Sallie, 38
Lippitt Sally Ash, 42
Lippitt Sam, 43
Lippitt Scofield, 42
Lippitt Selassie, 43
Lippitt Trilby Ash, 43
Lippitt Trixie, 38
Little Nugget, 81
Littletown Flirt, 100, 110, 114

Lone Pine Cajun, 115
Lord Clinton, 28
Lucille, 38
Lucinne, 38

Madrona Samantha, *37*
Madrona Trilby, *124*
Maestro, *see* Tarryall Gene
  Thiery
Magellan, 71
Maggie Marshall, 69
Major Antoine, 55
Major Gordon, 54
Major R. M., 59
Mansfield, 13, 30–3, 40, 42,
  55, 57, 58
Mansphyllis, 57, 58
Marches Gems Athena, 100
Marches Just Ethan, 100
May Rockwood, 59
Meade, 62
Mentor, 59, 61
Meredith Bilirubin, 37
Merry Ethan, 100
Michele's Desiree, 86, 95
Monnington Andante, 100,
  114, 115–17, 136
Monnington Aria, 105, 147
Monnington Bolero, 100
Monnington Calypso, 100,
  106, 109
Monnington Conductor, *95*,
  147–8, 149, 150
Monnington Descant, 83, 100,
  147, 150
Monnington Gamba, 146
Monnington Gershwin, *135*,
  146
Monnington Granados, 113,
  147, *148*, 149
Monnington Jubilate, 83, 85,
  86, 136, 147
Monnington Motif, 83, 100,
  147
Monnington Mozart, 100

Montabelle, 55
Montcrest Sellman, 55
Monte L, 59
Monterey, 58, 61
Mont Francis Claire, 134–5
Monty Vermont, 55
Moorewood Excalibre, 131
Morgan Woods Yankee, 144
Moro, 40
Moro Hill Gay Ethan, 55
Moro Hill's Emelyn, 99
Morril, 16, 69
Movement, 69
Mrs Culvers, 29
Mt Top Boomeran, 116, *117*
Mt Top Manitou, 116, 136,
  137

Naiad, 61
Nancy, 38, 40
Nekomia, 42
New Ran's Hawk, 144, *145*
Neva of Dickie, 109
Norfolk Shepherd, 69
Norma, 59
Novanna Ethan L, 100, 101,
  106, 110, 115

Old Green Mountain Morgan,
  see Hale's Green Mountain
Olympus Mr Promise, 107
Omar Shariff, 62
Onward, 69
Orland Leader, 34, 46, *47*
Orland Vigildon, 33–4, 46
Osogay, 62
Otter Brook Alida, *141*
Outrageous, 150

Panfield, 33
Panorama Pavanne, 146
Parade, 57, *58*, 95
Paragraph, 57
Parka, 59
Pat Allen, 55

Patrona, 55
Pecos, 46, *47*, 96, 11
Pegasus Royal Pride, 81, 84–6,
  87, 110, 125
Pennington Harlem, 147
Pennington Othello, 106
Penny Royal Trilight, 107
Penrod, 49, 50
Peter's Morgan, 15
Picture Perfect, 136
Piedmont Apache, 61
Plains King, 58
Polly Rogers, 38, 40
Primrose, 69

Querido, 32, 55, 59
Quietude, 33, 55, 59, 61, 71,
  95

Ranatha Stanhope, *142*, 143
Randolf Horse, 16
Rapidan Coquette, 85, 125
Rapid Road, 69
Raymond S. Sentney, 57
Rebelaire Satin, 116
Red Flash, 16
Redman, 55
Red Vermont, 50, 55
Redwood Morgan, 55
Revenge, 58
Revere, 58
Rienzi, 71–2
Rising Star, 69
Rising Star of the East, 69
Roan Allen F-38, 69
Robbins Night Flight, 97,
  104–5, 107, 109, 147
Robbins Top Duchess, 105,
  107
Rob Roy, 38, 40
Rockwood, 59
Rohan Camellia, 99
Rosco Morgan, 57
Rose B, 61
Rosefield, 59

157

Rose Mala, 59
Rosemeade, 62
Rose of Sutton, 38, 40
Royalton Ashbrook Darling, 43, 48
Royalton Ashline, 48, 99
Royalton Elenora, 48
Ruth, 33, 61

Saddleback Samantha, 111
Saddleback Silhouette, 146
Saddleback Supreme, 111
Schnuddel Mr Promise, 110, 125
Scotanna, 58
SGS Ability, *123*
Sealect, 38
See Jay Melody 81, 83–4, 85, 94, 116, 136
Select of Windcrest, 96
Senatefield, 59
Senator Graham, 59
Senator Knox, 59
Sentola, 105
She'll Do, 81
Shepard F. Knapp, 68
Sherman Morgan, 7, 12–13, 16, 68, 69
Silver Rockwood, 59
Sireson, 55
Sir Ethan Allen, 38
Sir Linsley, 57
Slect Passing Fancy, 113
Sockbridge Legacy, 111
Sonfield, 55, 59, 61
Sonoma, 61
Sorene, 136
South Forty Maid, 123
Sparbeau, 57
Sparhawk, 57
Sportsman, 3
Springervale Kristen, 95, 147
Springfield Lady Fair, 126

Starfire, 59, 94
Starwood Eclipse, 115
Stellar, 61
Sugar Run Ovation, 147, 149
Sun Down Morgan, 16
Sunflower Maid, 57
Supreme Command, 150
Susie, 38

Taproot Command Pilot, 103, *140*
Taproot Copper Iris, 102
Taproot Flagship, 103
Taproot Green Mt Boy, 102–3
Taproot Twin Flower, 103
Taproot Yankee Doodle, 102, 103
Tarheel Sweet Accord, 107, *108*
Tarryall Cadenza, 81, 82–3, 87, 147
Tarryall Gene Thiery, *iv*, *79*, 86–7, 95, 100, 106, 146, 147
Telegraph, 68
Ten Penny Action, 138
Thankyou Dearly, 147, 149
Thankyou Oh Wow, *149*
Thankyou Ovation, 147, *149*
Tiffany, 50
Tigre, 99
Tom Hal (Canadian), 70
Top Flight, 104, 105
Topside Jolly Roger, 81
Townsend First Edition, 109
Townsend Gaymeade, 62
Traveller, 10
Treelane Mystery Man, 126
Trijas Whiperpopper, 119
Trilby, 36, 42
Troubadour, 59
Troubadour of Willowmoor, 9, 33, 55, 59, *60*, 61
True Briton, 3, 10

Tyee, 59

U.C. Echo, 110, 114
U.C. Marquis, 100
U.C. Troubadour, 100
Ulendon, 32, 33, 34, 46, 47
Ulysses, 32, 33, 46, 62
Upwey Ben Don, 33, 34, 61, 94
Upwey Benn Quietude, 94
Upwey King Benn, 33, 95
Upwey King Peavine, 33
UVM Harmony, 138
UVM Promise, 107
UVM Titan, 121, *122*

Valiant Tony, 136
Verdonna Vermont, 55
Vigilda Burkland, 34, 47
Vigilendon, 34

Wanda, 59
Waseeka Firecracker, 94–5
Waseeka's Here Tiz, 94
Waseeka's Nocturne, 58, 59, 94
Washington, 69
W.A.W. Beau Heir, 119
Welcome, 38, 40
Whippoorwill Isis, 96
Whippoorwill Osiris, 96–7, 100, 115
Windcrest Sentimental Lady, 94
Wingo, 62
Woodbury Morgan, 8, 12, 13–15, 16
Woodstock Tabitha, 37

Young Woodbury, *see* Hale's Green Mountain